DEPTH
PSYCHOLOGY
AND
MODERN
MAN

Ira Progoff is the author of

THE CLOUD OF UNKNOWING (a modern rendering)

THE DEATH AND REBIRTH OF PSYCHOLOGY

DEPTH PSYCHOLOGY AND MODERN MAN

JUNG'S PSYCHOLOGY AND ITS SOCIAL MEANING

THE SYMBOLIC AND THE REAL

Depth Psychology & Modern Man

*A new view of the magnitude
of human personality, its dimensions
& resources*

Ira Progoff

McGraw-Hill Book Company

New York • St. Louis • San Francisco • Düsseldorf

Mexico • Montreal • Panama • São Paulo • Toronto

Author's note

Depth Psychology and Modern Man holds a position of pivotal importance in the development of techniques and disciplines for *evoking* the potentials of personality. It contains the background and structure of concepts that have led up to the various methods and programs of inner growth with which I have worked in recent years. Indeed, without this structure of concepts and the foundation of theory which it established, these practical programs could not have been conceived. In particular, the conception of *organic* process in the psyche as that conception was formulated in *Depth Psychology and Modern Man,* has provided principles that were absolutely essential in order that the *Intensive Journal* and its related techniques could be created.

The *Intensive Journal* is the specially structured psychological workbook that is used as the basic instrument in a variety of group workshops and individual programs of personal growth. It was originally developed as a practical extension of concepts presented in *The Symbolic and the Real,* and it has since become the corner-stone of Dialogue House programs in the fields of education, industry, religion, and social organization.*

The *Intensive Journal* is designed essentially to serve as a flexible means of objectifying the organic process by which the growth of personality proceeds. It is an instrument for mirroring these inner processes, for extending them, and eventually establishing a continuing relationship with them. This process is organic and natural, but it moves in cycles and by means of highly subjective thoughts and feelings. As a result, it is exceedingly difficult to mark off and identify just what the specific content and boundaries of this process are. It is very elusive, in part also because the form it takes is simultaneously

---

* See Progoff, *The Symbolic and the Real,* Julian Press, 1963, especially Ch. V; and also the Personal Growth workshop programs conducted by Dialogue House Associates, 45 West 10 Street, New York City.

general and individual. Its contents are universal in the sense
that they are true and are felt by all human beings, and they
are also unique in each person. The active functioning of this
process takes place *behind the mind* so that it is experienced
only at a level that is organically deeper than consciousness.
This increases the mercurial quality that makes it so difficult
to grasp. Considering that this elusive inner movement holds
the key to each person's growth, the *Intensive Journal* was
developed as the specific tool that would enable individuals
to get direct and definite access to the process so that they
could work with it constructively.

In one sense *Depth Psychology and Modern Man* is a theoretical and philosophical book. But the conceptual structure
developed in it is essential for understanding these practical
programs and the methodology for using them. To republish
this book in a new edition at this time is therefore of great
value, especially now that these active methods for evoking the
psyche are finding an increasing number of applications.

The contrast between the philosophical tone of this book
and its direct practical applications recalls to me the comment
made by an old friend shortly after *Depth Psychology and
Modern Man* was published. She expressed the wish that I had
started the book with the last three chapters and that I had
let the rest of the book follow after. If I had done that, she
said, she would have found her way to my theme and conclusions with much less difficulty. In fact she confided to me apol-
ogetically that she had almost not reached those last three
chapters, but once she had read them, she said, she was very
glad she had. Nonetheless, she wished I had made it easier for
her to get there.

I have reflected long about that comment. Could I indeed
have made my material more accessible to my readers? Possibly. And if it were possible, I certainly wish I had been able
to do it. Nonetheless, the thought remains with me that it was
altogether necessary to develop the conceptual structure first

in order that the deep principles that underlie the creative process could be seen in a large enough perspective. Only then would there be enough understanding of the quality of the principles involved to be able to apply them fruitfully. The organic processes involved here contain too great a dynamic for them to be used prematurely with incomplete understanding. They are of such a nature, I believe, that the results will amply repay the person who is willing to give them the time and attention they require.

Having said that, let me now add that the reader who wishes to skip ahead to the last three chapters is certainly free to do so. I am very sympathetic to the desire for speed, not to say haste, in this modern age; and I shall certainly forgive him. Only let him please bear in mind that it was the conceptual structure that preceded those last three chapters that made them possible at all, for that was the foundation on which they were built.

There are, it seems to me as I reflect on them now, several points in those last three chapters that are particularly significant in the light of events that have transpired in the decade since they were written. It has become more possible for us now to recognize that the work of creative research among scientists is profoundly subjective. We know now that basic discoveries in science are not brought forth by the rigid objectivity of rational calculation, as was formerly assumed. They come about through hunches, intuitions, and visionary experiences of diverse kinds. And they come especially from a total discipline of lifelong involvement in cultivating the capacity of subjective perception in order that it may be used creatively.*

People who live with an earnest life-commitment to scientific research are artists. Their research is their artwork. Just as is

---

* See Progoff, Ira. "The Humanic Arts" in *Forum for Correspondence and Contact,* October, 1968, and April, 1969. Here the conception of "disciplined subjectivity" is made the basis of a new approach to postgraduate education.

the case in any other field of art, the total personalities of creative scientists are involved in their work. This includes the height of their consciously developed talents and specialization together with the fullness of their deeper-than-conscious intuitive resources and sensitivities. To develop these inner sensitivities is essential for enlarging the capacities of scientific research. In Chapters 8 and 9 our references to such men as Bronowski, Kekule, and Pauli have the purpose of taking us into the actualities of creative experience. The section on *Depth Dynamics of Discovery* draws us into realms of experience that will be recognized by creatively involved persons who have been there. It will also serve to provide a model, a context, and guidelines for those who are engaged in devising the private psychological format that each individual requires to make possible a life of creative enterprise.

In this regard, I owe an apology to the readers of the first edition of *Depth Psychology and Modern Man*. On page 268 in a passage and footnote which still remain in the text, I indicated that more specific descriptions of the methods I was using would soon be published. As a result, numerous persons wrote to inquire when those publications would be available. These inquiries accumulated in a folder known to my office staff as the "Page 268 folder." It became a byword among us, and something for my associates to taunt me with.

The reason for this was simply that when it came time to publish the practical materials which I had promised, I felt a reluctance in myself to rush ahead with the formulation of a definite methodology lest anything be stated prematurely. Throughout the period of the late nineteen-fifties and the early nineteen-sixties, I was engaged in conducting group workshops using these principles and improvising with them in various experimental ways. The immediate responses were generally very good, and the long-range effects turned out to be exceedingly evocative in many persons. Over the years, I have received communications from a sizable number of persons to indicate that they identify major changes in the direction of their lives with their participation in one of those workshops.

At that time, however, I felt that something additional, some more specific refinement of the tools I was using, was required. I also felt the need to accumulate a larger amount of evidence and validation through the experimental use of a variety of approaches based on the organic process of the deep psyche. I did not wish to run the risk of putting a method into the public's hands before a full enough context and experience had been established. I therefore delayed publication of the materials I had promised on page 268.

In *The Symbolic and the Real,* published in 1963, I described some of the procedures for *evoking* the depth levels of the psyche that had been developed in the intervening period. This was presented in the context of Psyche-*Evoking* as a total approach to the active unfoldment of personality, a constructive alternative to the pathology-oriented techniques of *psychoanalysis.* In Chapter 5 of that book I also described the basis for a comprehensive and continuing program of personal growth utilizing the three primary relationships: 1) working alone in one's privacy; 2) working in a one-to-one dyad relationship; 3) participation in group workshops. That statement has served as the basis for subsequent programs developed by Dialogue House and implemented by numerous organizations across the country.

Among the major advances that have been made in this work since the publication of *The Symbolic and the Real* is the development of the "psychological workbook" into the structured form of *The Intensive Journal.* In this new format as an open-ended and yet disciplined workbook, *The Intensive Journal* lends itself to being used not only in the privacy of one's aloneness, but also in dyad relationships and in group workshops. Its combination of structure and flexibility has made it an invaluable tool. In the three years since it was developed, it has been used in a wide variety of situations both by myself and others. The results and testimonies of this usage have convinced me that this is the more specific tool I was still seeking in the years that followed the original publication of *Depth Psychology and Modern Man.* It contains the consolidation and crystallization of my varied experiences and searchings in individual and group work over the years.

To the many persons whose letters filled our "Page 268 folder," I can now finally give an answer in which I feel full confidence. It is that they test in their own experience the program of personal growth now maintained by Dialogue House in which techniques have been developed for the many-sided usage of *The Intensive Journal.* That program contains the practical application of the concepts and theoretical perspectives developed in this book.

One other point is important to mention in reintroducing *Depth Psychology and Modern Man.* This concerns its relation to theories of evolution, The vistas opened by the organic view of the psyche include spiritual transformations in human beings of such a nature as to suggest a next step in the evolution of our species. Especially during the past few years, it has been pointed out to me that the concepts and procedures presented here give modern western man a viable means, and therefore a realistic hope, of emerging successfully from his historical crisis and taking a major step forward in the development of the race. The implications of this, and the possibilities that it opens are of the greatest significance.

During the early nineteen-sixties when I was visiting in Switzerland at the Eranos Conference, I was struck by the fact that three different persons asked me whether I had used the work of the French Jesuit archeologist Pierre Teilhard de Chardin in writing *Depth Psychology and Modern Man.* They said that they found very deep and close affinities between that book and the underlying point of view which he presented. At that time I had to confess that I had no knowledge of his work. The cloud of suppression that covered Teilhard de Chardin in the early years had apparently hidden him from me. Since then, however, as English translations have appeared, I have had ample opportunity to gain a close and appreciative knowledge of his life and work. I find a particular connection between the overarching vision with which he studied evolution and the emergent conception of spirit that grows out of an organic approach to the depths of the psyche. The connection is integral, and it therefore seems that further developments and collaborations should be possible between the individuals interested in the two points of view.

Specifically, Teilhard de Chardin follows a large, open-ended approach to evolution. Through all the eons of time he sees it as moving up to man, then through man in order to go beyond him. He sees us all as participating in this unfolding process that carries the emergent meaning of life. In one sense this is a view of evolution that moves from matter to spirit. But that is merely a traditionalistic way of phrasing it. If I understand Teilhard correctly, he uses traditional language merely because that is where he was when he started his lifework. That was his only possible starting point. But a starting point is not only a place where one begins; it is also a place that one goes beyond. Indeed, that is the meaning of starting points. They are necessary beginnings, the goal of which is that they eventually be transcended and left behind.

Thus Teilhard moves through all the slow vastness of the cosmic past in order to reach what he designates as the *Noosphere,* which is essentially the human dimension, the reality and atmosphere of man's life. This atmosphere is the culmination of all that evolution has given, and it is the basis for all that is yet to come.

I find very close correspondences between this conception and the sensitivity to the unfoldment of life that one finds in such men as Jan Christian Smuts and Walt Whitman. It fits inherently with the tone of an organic depth psychology whose purpose is to provide tools and disciplines for the larger development of persons. It will be amply evident to the reader of this book that where I have referred to the holistic work of Smuts in building an evolutionary perspective, I could equally well have used the work of Teilhard de Chardin.

Their intent is the same. Each of them in his own conceptual framework sought to work out a large structural view of life in which individual human beings would be able to see both their smallness on the scale of the universe and the vastness of the possibilities inherent in their individuality. Both Smuts and Teilhard arrived at the reality of the person as the goal of all past evolution and as the beginning of evolutionary levels still to come. The question to which their work leads is the question of methods and disciplines by which it can become possible for persons so to develop their inner capacities that mankind will be taken beyond its present life of limitation and conflict.

Evolutionary thinkers like these set the basis and the perspective for such a step forward. They lead up to and call for a depth psychology of an organic, unitary, developmental type that will possess both empirical knowledge and intuitive understanding. Indeed, their lifeworks goad us to the realization that such a psychology is an urgent necessity in our time. Without it, man will continue to go around in the same circles that have led civilizations to their death again and again, and have prevented a further evolution in mankind. With it, man may eventually be able to take a definitive step beyond psychology, to transcend the cycles of history and give new evolutionary meaning to his existence. It is not an impossible hope.

IRA PROGOFF

August 1969
Dialogue House
New York City

Contents

DEPTH
PSYCHOLOGY
AND
MODERN
MAN

1 * The new depth psychology and the resources of personality

THE TRANSFORMATION OF THE UNCONSCIOUS

What is depth psychology? The phrase itself is forbidding, but suggestive too. To speak of depths awakens an image of something dark and hidden, of dimly lit caverns that may be dangerous to explore. But depths are also the places where treasures are hidden, and where, therefore, the most rewarding work of searching may be done.

These two images, of danger and discovery, give some indication of the ground that depth psychology covers. Its subject matter is the life of man, and the one observation that can safely be made about man's life is that it is a meeting ground of opposites. Tension and harmony, impasse and activity, despair and faith ever intermingle in human existence. It was so in the primal days when man first emerged from the animal kingdom; and it is still so now at the high point of civilization where we find ourselves in modern times, at once proud and uneasy. Man walks forward confidently toward ever new achievements, and all the while a sword of destruction is dangling over his head while a volcano of disturbance is slumbering within him.

We see the façades of personality on the surface where man meets his fellow man on a social level, and we know that this is not the fundamental ground of man's life. Something underlies it. Further back, in the hinterland of the self, something obscure but of great power is at work. How shall we understand what this something is? That is the undertaking of depth psychology.

In its goals and in its procedures, depth psychology is the very opposite of an analytic, segmental approach to man. Its subject matter is the human being, but depth psychology does not desire to become another one of the specialized sciences of man. It deliberately refrains from dissecting man and marking him off into compartments. It desires rather to comprehend man in his wholeness and so, when it studies the depth processes of personality, it maintains the perspective of man as a unity that is ever in process of growth. Depth psychology is now, at least in the conception of it that we shall present in this volume, *holistic* in the profound, integrative meaning that Jan Christian Smuts gave the term. And because it is holistic, it is able to meet the *existential* need of the modern situation. It addresses itself to the full range of human experience, from the impasses and frustrations of personal problems to the fullness of meaning that emerges at the creative edge of personality. In contrast to the analytic, diagnostic materialism of its earlier form, the new depth psychology is both *holistic* and *existential.*

The main characteristic of depth psychology's approach to the understanding of man is its emphasis upon searching out those factors that are active beneath the surface of behavior. It is especially interested in what has been called the *unconscious;* and it is the unconscious, defined and described in varying ways by the several schools of thought in depth psychology, that is most often called to mind when one speaks of "depth."

The *depth* in depth psychology pertains to the unconscious, or so it is most often assumed. But this has been changing significantly in recent years. The awareness of what the unconscious is and what the study of it implies has been growing steadily. Correspondingly, the appreciation of what depth is and what dimensions of experience it involves has been so enlarged that new vistas have opened in fields that were hardly known to the science of psychology before. Since the days when Sigmund Freud offered his pioneer theories about the unconscious, depth psychology has taken strides that have introduced a radically new conception of the unconscious, and especially of *depth.* It is these new vistas, which have transformed depth psychology since the early days of psychoanalysis, that we wish to explore here in order to reap the benefits of the new insights they make possible.

In its original meaning in depth psychology, *depth* was what Freud called the *unconscious repressed*. The traditional psychoanalytic understanding of this is that it refers to those mental contents that have been repressed or otherwise inhibited from reaching consciousness, and so remain at a lower level of the personality. They lurk in the unconscious and work surreptitiously in the background of events, often providing the secret motivation behind neurotic behavior. The depths of the psyche understood in this sense have essentially a negative aspect for they are conceived in terms of the pathology of personality.

The new developments in depth psychology have made it possible to approach the realm of *the unconscious* from an altogether different, an inherently affirmative and constructive point of view. The new holistic sense of depths is not conceived in terms of the malformations of personality, but rather in terms of what man's nature requires him to become. As with all animal species in evolution, the essential characteristic of the human organism is its spontaneous capacity for growth. Hidden in the depths of man there are indeed personal repressions and inhibitions of the kind Freud talked about; but of much greater consequence are the hidden propensities to growth which set the direction and provide the possibilities for human development.

As the oak tree lies hidden in the *depths* of the acorn, so the wholeness of human personality with its fullness of spiritual and creative capacities lies hidden in the *depths* of the incomplete human being silently waiting for its opportunity to emerge. The role and purpose of a holistic depth psychology are to describe the possibilities hidden in the depths of man, to ascertain the processes by which they unfold, and to devise practical procedures with which to expedite and enlarge the natural growth of personality.

It often happens that the potentialities in the individual do not wait silently for their opportunity to emerge but that they press, strain, clamor, disturb the entire personality until an avenue of expression is opened for them. Then depth psychology has the task of interpreting the tensions in a way that draws forth their constructive qualities so that the energy they have generated is not dissipated, but so that it works toward the fulfillment of personality.

Among the sciences available to modern man, depth psychology is uniquely able to undertake this task of guidance toward growth. It is capable of this because its underlying conceptions enable it to understand that the central frustration of modern man does not arise from his sexual repressions, as psychoanalysis long has taught, but rather that modern man suffers most from repressing those urgings at the core of his nature that require him to be a creative spiritual organism or to bear the marks of his insufficiency.

With this perspective we can readily see that the word *depth* in depth psychology has a much larger connotation than in its ordinary usage. It encompasses more than depths, it is heights as well. As an outcome of processes that take place in the depths of the psyche, a person may indeed reach the peaks of human experience. But all of this is contained in the special meaning of the word *depths* as it is used in depth psychology. It refers to the *magnitude* of human personality.

Depth is the dimension of wholeness in man. It is not a level in the psyche literally and spatially; but it is indeed a level in the human organism in *principle*. It is present and it is *deeper* down in the psyche in the sense that it is more fundamental than those mental contents that are in closer relation to surface consciousness and to sensory contact with the outer world. The depths contain what is implicit in the psyche, what is potential there, what is working in the background of individual development toward fulfillment by means of growth.

It should perhaps go without saying that the word *depths* is not to be interpreted in a literalistic way in terms of levels of space. Unfortunately, however, it is easy for people to fall into the habit of taking metaphoric phrases at their face meaning, with the result that their thinking becomes literal rather than fluid. This is one of the limitations of language, especially a limitation of the human beings who use language. It is a problem that arises particularly when language is being used simultaneously as a means of communication and as a tool of conceptual thinking. The two do not always fit well together because the unavoidable abstractness of conceptual thinking mitigates against the directness and simplicity necessary for good communication.

If we wish to reap the benefit of the advanced thinking in the field of depth psychology, it will be necessary that we bridge this gap—at least within our own minds. We have to resolve that we will not permit ourselves to interpret in a flat and literalistic way words that are being used metaphorically to communicate something that is true in principle and which, though its dynamic effect can be felt, is intangible and eludes the ordinary terms of description. This is a good discipline with which to teach the mind to think imaginatively so that it can participate in the poetry of intellectual search with a large and open vision.

It may help us in understanding the new, holistic meaning of *depth* if we follow the growth of its meaning historically. The term *depth psychology* was first used by the Swiss psychiatrist Eugen Bleuler in the early years of the twentieth century. It referred to the theory of the unconscious then being presented by Freud in terms of the "infantile wish" and its repression. Depth psychology then referred to the study of what takes place at the nonconscious levels of personality, and its conception of what the *depths* specifically contain was steadily expanded by authors in the first decades of the twentieth century, who built upon the base of Freud's original insights.

In this connection, we should keep in mind that when Freud wrote his first major and revolutionary book, *The Interpretation of Dreams,* its ultimate importance lay in something much more fundamental than the particular theory of dream interpretation he was presenting there. Today there is much discussion as to whether Freud's theory of dream interpretation was right or wrong; and when people conclude either that it was wrong or was seriously inadequate, they tend to reject Freud's psychologic approach as a whole. There is, however, something in the background that is most important to appreciate and to save. It is the seed of an insight that was planted by Freud; a potent seed which could not grow in the shades of his psychopathology. Given a larger, freer framework of thought, however, it will be able to bear its fruit and demonstrate what fertile intuitions Freud's first work contained.

What was truly significant in Freud's original book on dreams, and was in fact the fundamental revolutionary discovery that he was making, was not his special conception of the dream process with its theories of the unconscious wish, infantile sexuality, and the pathologic aspects of the depths of man. It was, rather, his recognition that there are processes taking place beneath the surface of awareness and that these processes are as real, as subject to law, and to scientific principles of understanding, as the processes of the body. This was the basic insight and conception that Freud brought forth. His interpretation of dreams was a special aspect of this, for he understood dreams as one particular manifestation of the depth processes of the psyche, just as myths, paintings, poems, and ultimately all the creative activities of the human psyche are also.[1]

[1] See the excellent new edition of Freud's *The Interpretation of Dreams* published by Basic Books, Inc., in 1956 with a new translation by James Strachey. The completeness of this volume with its annotations makes it of very great value in the study of the history of depth psychology. Editorially it is on a par with the exceptionally fine volumes being produced by the Bollingen Foundation in *The Collected Works of C. G. Jung* (New York, Pantheon Books). These are also indispensable in studying the history of depth psychology.

It was Freud's conception of the reality of the psychic processes underlying man's conscious activities, not his special interpretations constructed in terms of neurosis, that provided the basis for the later work of Otto Rank and especially of C. G. Jung. In this sense the general description of a dimension of psychic depths in man, regardless of its specific characteristics, was certainly the most fundamental part of Freud's pioneering; for it eventually played a seminal role in the post-Freudian study of man.

Once one takes the idea of unconscious processes seriously and really works with it, it becomes rather obvious that the dynamic force active at the deep levels of the psyche must involve something more than simply the repressed personal material of which Freud spoke. Freud himself felt this. It might be then—and this was Jung's hypothesis—that the basic psychic processes are essentially formative patterns, tendencies toward particular styles of life and of growth comparable in man to the tendency toward nest-building in birds, or the tendency toward social organization among certain insects.

In man the primary formations that are the equivalent of innate patterns of behavior among animals are to be found in the great mythologies and ideologies, the great symbolic structures of meaning that provide the frames of reference in terms of which civilizations can live. These underlying symbolic patterns are expressed in many varieties of imagery. Dreams and fantasy are one form; poetry, painting, and religious experiences are other forms; and the depth visions of reality upon which such scientists as Kepler and Einstein based their studies are still another form. But more important than the specific forms of symbolism is the fact that the underlying tendencies and patterns of behavior in man are expressed in processes that are inherent in the psyche, deeply implanted in man's organic nature. And these processes move forward out of the depths of the psyche toward the unfoldment and wholeness of the human organism.

The motifs or themes underlying the patterns of symbolism that belong to the process of growth in the psyche have been studied by Jung under the term *archetypes,* and by Rank, with a more historical and less universalistic emphasis, as the *prototypes.* The work of Jung and Rank in this direction has involved a profound extension of the original conception of depths as the repressed material in the unconscious. It went far beyond Freud, both in its content and in its implications, and yet it grew directly out of the seeds that Freud had planted. In a later section of this book, we shall have an opportunity to place these important contributions of Jung and Rank in the context of new biologic conceptions, in order to emerge with a fuller understanding of the *organic psyche* in man and the varieties of *protoplasmic imagery.*[2]

DEPTH AS THE DIMENSION OF WHOLENESS IN MAN

The development of thought in depth psychology has now come far from Freud's original version of psychic depths

[2] See Chapters VI and VII.

as the unconscious repressed. It has in fact gone full circle from the psychoanalytic diagnosis of man in his illness and incompleteness to a view of *wholeness in depth* as the most adequate way to understand the magnitude of human nature.

The human organism unfolds in the course of its growth toward maturity as an acorn becomes a tree. It moves unknowingly, and yet with a significant development of consciousness along the way, toward a purpose that is inherent in its nature, a purpose contained in the seed of what it is its nature to become. What guides the unfoldment of the whole person is the unconscious psychic processes. Processes of this magnitude and power, capable of carrying out this encompassing integrative function in the human organism, cannot conceivably be derived from the small personal repressions as Freud's theory first presumed. Their source must rather be something that is nonpersonal in the individual, something that is there generically by virtue of the fact that he is a human being, and that therefore the natural processes universal in mankind are working toward fulfillment in him.

This is the sense in which depth is the dimension of wholeness in man. Wholeness is not given to man complete and final. It is given to him rather as a possibility, as something that can become an actuality if it is able to grow and fulfill itself. The essence of depth then is growth, growth toward wholeness. And it is the business of depth psychology firstly to describe the processes by which this growth strives to take place in man; and secondly, to devise procedures of work by depth principles that can achieve growth toward wholeness in modern man even in the midst of the perpetual crisis in which he lives.

The task that depth psychology has before it is that of finding and developing these resources of modern man that can be of use to him in his present time of troubles. These are not economic resources, nor are they political resources. They are essentially resources of human personality that have been permitted to spoil in neurosis simply for lack of creative use.

In modern times the economic and political sides of life have been developed to a high degree, but that is just where the problem begins. Modern society has concentrated upon the externals of existence, upon industrial production, high standards of consumption, and upon those mechanistic aspects of the mind that can be manipulated by advertising and planned propaganda. Concentrating the attention outside, a vacuum has developed within.

One of the outstanding tragedies of modern society has been its disregard for the creative component of individuality. There is a profound and disturbing paradox here, for Western civilization has truly been founded upon its appreciation of the uniqueness and the dignity of the individual in all areas of life. Western civilization has so valued this that it has traditionally considered its appreciation of human personality to be one of its main contributions to history. And yet the fact remains that modern man's conception of himself has been hollowed out, leaving emptiness where a creative spirit might have been expected to be. The outcome of modern man's achievements in scientific discovery is that he has learned enough about "deterministic" laws to have contempt for his own capacities of freedom, so that he now thinks of himself as a cipher.

At the present point in civilization, the modern person is treated not as a spiritually creative being, but as an object. He is treated, in the phrase of Martin Buber, not as a *Thou* (a person) but as an *it* (a thing); and he behaves that way as well. For that is the worst of it. The modern person tends to think of himself as though he actually were a *thing,* as though he actually were determined by the same mechanical laws that govern his television set and his refrigerator. This is the most serious aspect of the situation, for it means that by now the modern person has become subtly acclimatized to looking outside himself for his supports. Now modern man does not turn to himself, nor does he attempt to develop his inner capacities. He sees no reason even to attempt to do so, for he has been led to believe that the source of creativity does not lie within him.

The work of depth psychology proceeds upon an exactly opposite assumption. Its underlying conception is that man is not an empty being, but that he is inherently a creative one. There is indeed a living seed in man, a seed of growth; yes, a seed of divinity. The primary problem before us is how we can help that seed mature into a fruitage consonant with the rich possibilities of its nature.

The particular hypothesis with which holistic depth psychology does its work is that the seed of growth, the seed of creativity, the seed of divinity in man are one and the same. They are not separate from one another. And

further, the processes by which this seed comes to fulfillment arise out of man's natural condition as a being in the
animal kingdom. These processes have a spiritual outcome
when they are able to fulfill themselves, but they proceed
by psychologic principles. These are the principles that
are the main province of depth psychology, for the purpose of depth psychology is to uncover them, to interpret
them, and to develop the practical procedures by which
they can be brought to a successful spiritual outcome in
the situation of modern times.

The processes of growth with which depth psychology is
concerned are the processes by which what is potential in
man progressively becomes more real, more actual, so that
the meaning of man's life as a spiritual being in the
natural world and in history is fulfilled in the individual's
existence.

A major change has been taking place in the focus of
modern thinking during the past decade. The Western interest in the oriental approach to religion and the recent,
long overdue awakening of existential awareness in the
United States are signs of this. Correspondingly, it has
been my pleasure to find during the past year that persons
who would have been horrified at the mere mention of
such a text as *The Cloud of Unknowing* not very long ago
are now ready to consider what such religious existential-
ism has to offer. Those whose range of thinking has been
circumscribed by the rationalistic philosophies that derived from the eighteenth century or who have been satu-
rated with nineteenth-century materialism and scientifi-
cism now are beginning to realize that there is something

in the universe even more meaningful than rationality. And realizing this, they have to take the necessary step of opening themselves to the nonrational aspects of human existence.

There are many people indeed who have been forced to recognize that the rationalistic conception of man is not all that they had thought it to be. They have experienced a disillusionment in their faith in reason; but for most of them it can be said that they have not yet found a new faith. They do not know yet where their new answer lies, nor even what form it will eventually take. But they are engaged in the act of searching. They are reaching, and psychologically this is the first step toward a valid existential experience.

It may seem at first glance that there are important differences in the qualities of this reaching. Those who have been accustomed to think of the world in terms of rationalistic concepts do not find it easy to come quickly to a sense of the immediacy of God, or a living feeling of unity with the infinite in creation. Neither can they easily feel at home in the labyrinths of irrational symbolism that are explored by depth psychology as it searches for threads of eternal truths in the dark abysses of the human psyche. There are great and basic differences of point of view and habits of thinking. And yet something is taking place within the transformations of modern thought and in the modern quest for larger dimensions of meaningful experience that seems to reach beyond the differences. It may be that, once the old foundations of belief have been shaken strongly enough, a common spiritual experience transcending doctrinal differences actually becomes possible.

In very many areas of his life, the experience of modern man has brought him to a situation in which he can no longer feel content with his old view of himself, of man in general, and of the meaning of life. He has lost his confidence in the conceptions he took for granted in the past. He now is bereft of his old beliefs, of the old slogans that provided readily available meanings for his life in the past. He therefore finds himself in a position that is most difficult, especially from an ideologic point of view. From a personal point of view, too, it is most uncomfortable; for it has left the modern personality without the sustenance of faith, either secular or spiritual, that the individual requires.

Modern man is indeed in a difficult psychologic situation because of the loss of his old cultural and religious faiths; but paradoxically it is also a healthy condition and one that holds considerable possibility for growth. The old beliefs no longer work for him. We see this expressed in the breakdown of morality in personal affairs, in political and economic life, and in the whole fabric of modern living. The individual is no longer able to call upon the resources of his culture to sustain him in his personal life. He is forced rather to turn into himself, to search within himself for resources with which to carry on his life.

He is forced to do this even if he is one of those individuals who are not inclined by temperament (or by what we would call "psychological type") to undertake the kind of discipline and to maintain the attitude toward oneself that the work of inner search requires. Very often, especially in the past two generations, individuals in modern society have literally been forced to pay attention to their inner life because they were unable to function in the outer world. This failure of adaptation has been diagnosed as neurosis under various headings; and under its impact many a modern individual who had been well convinced of the supremacy of the materialistic view of life and of outer, seemingly objective reality has found himself forced to recognize the very surprisingly strong and valid realities of the inner life.

When the individual realizes that he cannot achieve a productive life by straining to adapt himself to society, since society itself is confused, he is thrown back upon himself. His main resource then is nothing else than his own being. At first his experience of this is one of great pain, of loneliness, an absence of social support. He feels this lack in a form that carries the symptoms of neurosis. The breakdown of old symptoms and beliefs gives the individual a sense of isolation and anxiety, which might be spoken of as a personal feeling of cosmic isolation. But that passes when the individual is able to realize that the great treasure house of resources for his life has always been within the individual person. Now that the difficulties of modern life have broken down the easy roads of social adaptation, the individual is forced back to the realization of an ancient truth which Western civilization has permitted itself to forget: the realization that the basic resources for life are contained within the human personality.

A SCIENCE FOR EXISTENTIAL GROWTH

With this insight we are in a position to understand the historic significance of the fact that depth psychology has arisen as a disciplined field of scientific study in modern times. Other kinds of psychology study man's perceptions, his sensations, his nervous system, his ways of learning, remembering, and forgetting. But depth psychology addresses itself to those processes of personality that govern the ultimate experiences of man's life. It delves into the question of what people really believe beneath their conscious avowals of faith. It investigates what people really desire beyond the things that society tells them they want. And depth psychology undertakes to provide methods of individual study and work to clarify and crystallize the processes of thought and decision active at the unconscious levels of personality. In a period of history that is characterized by a social and psychologic flux so rapid that people do not have an opportunity to discover what is in their minds and hearts, such a study speaks to the urgent needs of the time.

When depth psychology began to gain attention in modern civilization, its first major form was in the medical conceptions of Freudian psychoanalysis. We can see now at this date in the history of depth psychology that the medical view was not in a position to clarify the basic problems of belief and meaning in life about which the modern person was confused. Indeed, psychoanalysis negated the entire question with a severe psychologizing relativism, a sweeping medical nihilism of the soul. The Freudian way of approach, especially in the first periods of psychoanalytic work, reduced beliefs and meanings in life to unconscious wishes, obsessive compulsions, and other neurotic symptoms.

It is very pertinent for us to ask why psychoanalysis was able to reduce the meaning of life to a medical symptom and have so large a proportion of modern educated people accept the diagnosis. Part of the answer must certainly include the observation that many of the people who accepted the viewpoint of psychoanalysis had already lost their faith in the various beliefs that psychoanalysis was now diagnosing. And this would include many simple and basic attitudes ranging from observance of the Sabbath and church attendance to dancing, the theater, the changed attitude toward entertainment, and the new flexibility in sexual relationships.

Freud's basic psychoanalytic research was carried out in the midst and very largely under the impact of this transformation of social attitudes. As a medical man he daily encountered in his consultation room individuals who were not able to function in their social environment, and he considered their problems as sympathetically and as honestly as he could. When he studied the symptoms, however, he saw them all in the light of problems of sexuality.

Certainly the problems of sexuality were there, and were right at the forefront. It had to be so, since the major social change of the period concerned the weakening of the traditional forms of family life and the transformation of moral codes of behavior. Approaching the symptoms as a medical man trained in neurology, Freud quite understandably saw the etiology in biologic, especially instinctual terms. But the underlying source of the problems he was seeking to treat lay on the social level where the symbols that had carried the meanings of life and the guiding principles of conduct had broken down.

At another pole of depth psychology during the early days of its development, Alfred Adler looked at the same symptoms and saw not sexuality but competitiveness. He was looking at another aspect of the breakdown of social symbols. The beliefs that had broken down in the nineteenth century under the impact of the new industrial society had previously served as a kind of social cement; they had held social life together. Most important, they had given the individual a feeling of connection to the rest of the community. This was what Adler spoke of as *social feeling*. He was especially sensitive to the absence of *social feeling* in modern times, for he realized that it is a basic ingredient without which human culture cannot continue to function. But Adler was also a medical man, and his habit of diagnosis persisted. He pin-pointed the modern problem as a lack of *social feeling,* a lack which he felt to be expressed in the competitiveness of modern society and in its self-pampering pursuit of the pleasure principle.

Of the early depth psychologists, C. G. Jung has perhaps made the diagnosis historically most true. He placed the emphasis altogether on the breakdown in the experience of meaning in the modern world, and his conception of therapy is essentially an attempt to overcome the effects of this breakdown. It became, in Jung's frame of reference, not merely a question of social belief but of the inner experience of social symbols that relate the individual to the continuity of the past of his culture. It is Jung's enduring contribution that, in the history of depth psychology, he was the first author to treat the question of religious experience not merely as a psychologic datum, as a psychologic symptom to be diagnosed, but as a valid and authentic part of the human personality.

The contact with religious facts—not conscious creeds and dogmatic observances, but the inner relatedness of the individual to basic experiences of the reality of life—was to Jung of central importance in the growth and functioning of the human being. It was to him not a symptom of something but a fact in itself. In his view of things, therefore, the breakdown of basic religious and historical symbols was not merely a symptom of modern man's troubles but it was the trouble itself.

This line of thinking has led to very provocative conjectures. If modern man is ill because his basic symbolic beliefs about life have lost their hold upon him, we are led to the implication that his psychologic health would be restored to him if he could manage to experience once again the reality of the old symbols as he had in the past. But this is a very large question. Is it true that if the old traditional faiths were restored to their earlier positions of primacy modern man would be healed?

Oddly enough, it may be that exactly the opposite is the case. It may indeed be that this is our greatest fortune in modern times. In the fuller perspective of history we may one day come to realize that the most fortunate thing that happened to man in the modern age was that his symbols broke apart. When that happened he was cut off from the traditional resources of his culture and his first reaction was to think that he was ill. He was indeed acting as though he were ill, but something much more significant was taking place in the background. With the collapse of his framework for social contact, he was thrown back upon the fundamental root and ground of his own being.

The breakdown of traditional symbolism opened a large road of discovery for modern man, but his first reaction to it was confusion: it led to a certain disorder, even turmoil, in his personal behavior, and this was analyzed medically with great clinical skill. This has, in fact, provided the source materials for the pioneer studies in depth psychology, and has led to large new insights into the nature of human personality and its problems in the modern world.

In fundamental ways the history of depth psychology has shown a steady enlargement of understanding on this question. To Freud the breakdown of social symbols revealed itself simply as neurotic symptoms. To Adler it disclosed itself as a violation of man's inherent social nature. And to both C. G. Jung and Otto Rank it opened an awareness of that basic Self in man that exists prior to all symbols.

Here Jung and Rank, each in his own way, came into contact with the flow of imagery that is fundamental to the functioning of the psyche and is the source of meaning in man's experience.[3] But this would not have been possible for them if the functioning of the social symbolism on the conscious level had not become so disturbed in modern man that the inchoate symbolism of the psychic depths was thrust up to the surface where it could be studied. It was this encounter with unguarded elements of the deep psyche that has suggested dynamic procedures of personality development that may well open a new way to creative experience beyond self-consciousness and psychologic analysis.

To retrace the growth of insight in depth psychology in this way leads to a fuller understanding of its role in modern times. *The history of depth psychology embodies the existential situation of modern man.* It has provided a full-length reflection of the problems of personality for the past fifty years, and as such it has been one of the most sensitive expressions of the predicament of our times. The very fact that there is a depth psychology today is an outcome of the fact that traditional frameworks of belief have lost much of the strength they had in generations past. And with the new awareness that depth psychology is achieving, we are now able to see the affirmative possibilities inherent in a situation that might well have been thought to be the spiritual disaster of modern man.

Now, let us ask, what is it that depth psychology in its newly emergent form can give to modern man? Can it give him a new system of beliefs to replace the old faiths that have fallen apart? It will not do that. Deliberately it will

[3] See Chapters VI, VII, VIII.

not do that, for it is not a philosophy. Depth psychology undertakes to provide not beliefs but a practical knowledge of man conceived in the spirit of science. It does not espouse any particular faith; and it does not negate any particular religious doctrine as such. It moves on another level, considering that what a person *professes* to believe or what he *thinks* he believes is not as important as what he actually experiences. Depth psychology turns its attention to the more fundamental level, the level of *experience* that underlies belief. It seeks to provide, upon the basis of empiric knowledge, first an understanding of the principles of experience that underlie faith; and second, a knowledge of practical methods by which an encounter with the meaning of life can become a real possibility upon a psychologically valid foundation. Depth psychology is concerned, therefore, not with new doctrines for modern man, but with providing *ways of experience* by which each person, according to his individual nature, can relate himself in actuality to the ultimate realities of life.

In a recent, exceedingly cogent article in *The Saturday Evening Post*,[4] Paul Tillich spoke of a "lost dimension in religion." "Without knowing what has happened to him," Tillich wrote, modern man "feels that he has lost the meaning of life, the dimension of depth." [5] What remains is religious belief upon a "horizontal plane," that is, the literalized, secularized understanding of religious symbols with the richness of mystery and meaning washed out of them. What remains is rationalistic, flat, and superficial.

[4] June 14, 1958.
[5] *Ibid.*, p. 78.

For example, Tillich writes, "If the symbols of the Sav-
iour and the salvation through Him which point to the
healing power in history and personal life are transferred
to the horizontal plane, they become stories of a half-
divine being coming from a heavenly place and returning
to it. Obviously, in this form, they have no meaning what-
soever for people whose view of the universe is determined
by scientific astronomy."[6]

This describes very well the situation of modern man
emptied of his traditional beliefs and left without a point
of contact for a meaningful life. But what can be done for
him? Tillich understands very well that religious acts carried out upon the "horizontal plane" are futile. "The real
answer," he says, "to the question of how to regain the
dimension of depth is not given by increased church
membership or church attendance, nor by conversion, or
healing experiences." These are of no use because they do
not involve the depth of the person. But the answer is
given, Tillich maintains, "by the *awareness* that we have
lost the decisive dimension of life, the dimension of depth,
and that there is no easy way of getting it back." [7] (My
italics).

Here, however, a problem arises, and from it we can see
how the new holistic depth psychology fulfills the goals of
the existential philosophers. Tillich's suggestion for overcoming the loss of the "dimension of depth" in modern
man is simply the awareness of the loss itself; for, Tillich
writes, "He who realizes that he is separated from the ulti-

[6] *Ibid.*, p. 78.
[7] *Ibid.*, p. 79.

mate source of meaning shows by this realization that he is not only separated but also reunited."

Tillich is certainly correct in this statement, at least *in principle:* but the recovery of the dimension of depth in modern man is a *practical* question. When Tillich speaks of "awareness" he obviously means much more than a mere intellectual awareness. He means a realization that is experienced with a shaking strength and intensity in the nonrational depths of the person. What can make that happen? If persuasive philosophic arguments could restore the dimension of depth to modern man, it would have been accomplished long ago. And similarly, if it were within the power of theological systems to make spiritual realization a fact, the need would already have been met for modern man many times over. But that is just where the problem lies. Concepts will not do it. Impressive intellectual pronouncements will not do it. Even profound insights in religious history will not do it, though all of these may help.

Ultimately what is necessary is a *practical way of working.* Modern man requires a knowledge of the principles and procedures by which an inner experience of reality can be achieved. This is the practical side of the goals that such existential authors as Paul Tillich and Martin Buber have set before modern man; and depth psychology in its holistic form, conceiving man as an organism of psychologic depth and of spiritual magnitude, is the one disciplined branch of science that is making an earnest attempt to meet this need.

This new kind of depth psychology has an important

contribution to make in several areas of the life of modern man. Most fundamentally, it brings a conception of human nature that restores man's feeling of a creative power working within him. It provides the understanding and the procedures with which the sense of the spiritual can be reawakened in modern man. While philosophers and theologians may eloquently recommend religious experience, the new depth psychology undertakes to do something concrete about it. It works with practical methods toward the wholeness of personality in the individual, thus to make religious experience psychologically possible in the modern disenchanted mind.

This goal of wholeness and of the spiritual growth of personality gives an emphasis that is quite different from the medical orientation with which analytic depth psychology has worked in the past. Wholeness means not only the healing of pathology but the fulfillment of the potentialities of the human person. It means opening up and drawing upon the psychologic resources in the depths of man reaching toward an experience of meaning. Holistic depth psychology is thus oriented truly toward what man can become as a being aware of the dimension of depth in his existence.

The goal of wholeness is central for the new depth psychology, but it has a number of additional aspects. One of the most important of these is the techniques it suggests for assisting the creative process by working in the depth of the psyche. These may be of value for artists and writers, for persons engaged in the activities of social and business life, and for creative scientists engaged in the tasks of discovery. We shall have an opportunity to see some examples of this later in this book.

Depth psychology in its new holistic form is the branch of science that provides the practical tools with which modern man can restore the dimension of depth to his existence. This is indeed an important role of great spiritual significance if it can be fulfilled. There is much to be done in clarifying the concepts of such a science, and in indicating the areas in which it can be fruitfully applied. In the chapters that follow, we undertake to move in that direction. We investigate the background of depth psychology, the development of thought that has led it to its present position, and its relation to other sciences, especially to biology. Upon the basis of this, we shall describe some of the fundamental conceptions with which holistic depth psychology works, so that we can appreciate its role in theory and practice as an existential tool for individual growth in the life of modern man.

2 * The depth dimension in the study of man

THE EARLIEST SOURCES: PSYCHE AND COSMOS

As a science, depth psychology is of relatively recent vintage; but the roots of its conception of man reach far back into the religions and philosophies of ancient times. Even in the earliest periods of history there were men who studied the nature of the human mind in a serious, objective, and insightful way. Such men as Empedocles, Heraclitus, and the semimythical men who molded the world view of the ancient Orient must be included among these; for they understood the mind of man as a dynamically creative entity with hidden realms far beneath the surface, and with a capacity for reaching out into life in intangible and wonderful ways. With them we have already in embryo the conception of the magnitude of human personality that is a cornerstone of modern depth psychology.

Within the context of Western civilization, particular credit must be given to the heroic predecessors of Socrates for their contribution to the depth understanding of man. This is so on several counts. For one thing, such fabled pre-Socratics as Pythagoras, Parmenides, and Democritus, in addition to Empedocles and Heraclitus, left an enduring mark upon Plato, especially the older Plato, and the Neo-Platonic lines of thought that followed him; and through this the sense of depths in man together with a feeling for the extensiveness of the human spirit remained as a continuing though seldom dominant current in Judaeo-Christian thought.

A second important factor, which is an outcome of this continuity, is that in the years of the Enlightenment, the pre-Socratics were rediscovered by European philosophers. Especially Heraclitus exerted an influence that has reached through Schopenhauer, Nietzsche, and von Hartmann into the heart of modern depth psychology in the conceptions of Freud, and especially those of Jung and Rank.

Perhaps the keynote of what is important in the pre-Socratics is expressed in the phrase of Heraclitus that the human personality "has no boundaries." Stated affirmatively and transposed into modern terms, this would mean that human life has aspects in which it reaches beyond itself, that there are illimitable dimensions in man by which man is connected to the cosmos in more ways than he knows; and the central means of this connection is his

psyche. The illimitable magnitude of the human personality in all the forms in which it is experienced by the individual expresses the ontological, the metaphysical core
of life in which the human and the cosmic are essentially
one.

This sense of the extensiveness of human nature, its
depths and its reaches, has dwindled in the modern mind;
and the lack of it is one of the main reasons for the modern feeling of personal emptiness. We shall have occasion
to discuss this condition and its implications from several
different vantage points in later pages. But we should not
pass it by here without remarking that eminent scientists
in both the psychologic and the physical fields are increasingly calling attention to this very fact: the importance of
the inner connection between human nature and the ultimate nature of the cosmos. It is a question that arose in
older contexts of philosophy; but it arises again with new
meaning at the most advanced outposts of modern science.

A significant instance of this is a recent paper delivered
by Gardner Murphy, in which he undertook to relate the
findings of the embryologist Spemann and the biologist
von Bertalanffy to the study of the human personality. Reporting on the results of their researches in the field of
the life sciences, Murphy pointed to the weight of evidence indicating that the basic patterns of form and structure are repeated throughout the universe, and that they
are equally, in his phrase, "duplicated in man." [1]

[1] "Main Currents in Modern Thought," September, 1956. See also Dr.
Murphy's provocative book, *Human Potentialities*, New York, Basic Books,
1958.

Drawing upon these observations, Murphy goes on to say that the human being may be understood in these terms as a universe in miniature, which repeats, "like the sympathetic vibration of a wire, the vaster processes of the macrocosm." For, as he states it, "the nature of man may be seen . . . as a replica of larger forces."

From this Murphy draws two reversible inferences. The first is that, being a replica of the universe, man may be able to understand something of his own nature by studying the nature of the cosmos: and conversely, by penetrating more deeply into his own nature, man may be able to comprehend more about the nature of the universe. For, Murphy says, "the boundaries that separate us as individuals one from another, and as humans from the cosmos . . . are often less sharp than we imagine."

These remarks are the observations of a psychologist interpreting the results of advanced physical scientists. Is it not significant then that the culminating insight he reaches, as expressed in the last sentence we cited above, strongly recalls the saying of Heraclitus from which we have already quoted, "No matter what road you follow, you will not reach the limits of the soul; for the soul has no boundaries."

It does indeed seem that this is the outcome man is destined to reach in his thinking "no matter what road" he follows, whether it is the road of philosophy or the road of science. These two roads seem to be converging in the realization that when man studies himself in depth, he shows himself to be a mirror of the universe with respect both to his intellectual knowledge and his spiritual experience. But, though it seems to be an eventual outcome, the task of penetrating the human personality in a way that will develop this capacity for "mirroring" the universe and will draw forth its implications for our understanding of life has been sadly neglected until now in modern thinking. Depth psychology stands alone as the branch of science that has turned its attention to amplifying the human side of this man/cosmos relationship in a disciplined way. And it has been able to undertake this because its basic working hypothesis is a conception of the illimitableness of human personality as an organism in nature, a conception that has much in common with the profound view of man that made its first appearance in the distant days of the pre-Socratic philosophers.

PSYCHOLOGY IN THE CONTEXT OF WESTERN THOUGHT

An awareness of the depth dimension of the psyche was a cornerstone of the classical age of Greek philosophy, especially in the thought of Plato and the various traditions of thought that derived from him. Subsequently, however, the understanding of man's psychologic nature underwent many transformations.

In the age of the Stoics, the study of man assumed a more sophisticated, world-weary style. The subterranean levels of the mind were not forgotten, but life itself was approached with a detached, intellectual attitude of a kind that was to recur in a later century with the insights of Montaigne.

Significantly, during the same years in which the Stoics flourished, there was also a widespread experience of the reality of the nonrational levels of the psyche expressed in a diversity of religious forms, varying from the rites of the Greek mystery religions to the visions and exaltations of the Jewish Apocalyptics. This was a period of history in which the symbolic dimension of human experience was felt to be profoundly real in its own right. It was a time, therefore, when the "depth" or "unconscious" level of the psyche could not be described in terms of an intellectual construct. It did not need to be, for it was lived spontaneously and intensely as the self-evidently valid content of life, the common ground of experience in an age of great spiritual turmoil.

In those transitional centuries, history was literally being made in the depths of the psyche. The Mediterranean world was then the scene of the great trauma in Western civilization, the outcome of which was the birth of the Christian era. It was indeed a profound psychologic trauma and it extended culturally over a protracted period of time. The painful birth of Christendom covered many generations as it moved northward in Europe and it reached deeply into the psyche because the basic transformation that was taking place belonged to the realm of symbolic spiritual experience.

The question of the acceptance or rejection of the new Christian doctrines could not be settled on the level of conscious intellect, but ultimately had to be referred to the nonconscious depths for judgment. The early Christian authors could not fail to have an active awareness of the largeness and importance of the deep psyche as the central ground where man works out his living relation to God, for this was the field of their own experiences. Men like Augustine were engaged in an original and creative enterprise, the ultimate goal of which was to develop an intellectual point of view capable of carrying the new spiritual message to the pagan European mind.

Early Christian thinking drew upon both the Greek and the Jewish wisdoms, and so it proceeded with an informed sensitivity to the depths of the psyche. As the years passed, however, this ancient capacity for spiritual understanding was increasingly hemmed in by the growing body of clerical dogma, and especially by the tendency to interpret literally rather than spiritually the heaven-centered symbolism that gradually emerged as the frame of reference for the medieval mind.

The rise of the authoritarian point of view in the Christian Church had a major and inhibiting effect upon the knowledge of the depths of the psyche with which Christianity had begun. Much that had been known was forgotten, was irreparably hardened into dogma, or was lost by being transformed into rigid theological constructs that did not contain the feeling of free flow and movement essential for the living experience of the depths of personality. What we speak of here as the psyche was regarded as the exclusive province of the established religious orthodoxy. Only theologians were authorized to interpret what takes place in the mind and spirit of man, and this attitude was a serious blow to the awareness of the depths of human nature that had been a legacy to Western civilization from the ancient philosophers.

In time the theological restrictions on the study of the psyche were lifted so that, by the beginning of the modern intellectual era, professional philosophers as well as theologians were considered competent to comment on the inner life, the soul, and the mind. Man's understanding of himself was then radically transformed. As it had first been used as a tool of philosophy in the classic period of Greece and Rome, and as it had dwindled when used as a tool of theology in medieval Europe, the study of psychology returned to prominence again in early modern times as part of the resurgence of philosophic inquiry. It played an important role in forming the great new tradition in modern philosophy which began with Descartes and continued through Locke, Berkeley, and Hume to Kant and the psychologic philosophies of the twentieth century.

This direction in philosophy in which the interest in the psyche holds a pivotal position may be understood as an intellectual attempt to discover and define the meaning of life for European man as he stood on the brink of the modern era. In doing so, it challenged and discarded many of the conceptions of life that had been fundamental in the older religious view of the world. In particular, it undertook to find the values and meanings for life that modern man required by studying minutely the nature and limitations of man's capacity for knowledge. The modern trend in philosophy thus studied the psychologic functioning of man, but it did so from a severely intellectualistic point of view.

As part of this development, it came about that studies of the psychologic nature of man were first carried forward in modern times as attempts to find answers for philosophic problems. Within the framework of epistemology there were resolutely critical inquiries into what man believes he knows, how he knows, and how knowledge is possible for man at all. And there were also, accompanying this rationalistic epistemology, philosophic studies of man's nonrational faculties, his passions, sentiments, and sympathies. These various inquiries, conducted in the light of seventeenth- and eighteenth-century philosophy, were precursors of the more specialized psychologic investigations carried on in the European universities of the nineteenth century, which eventually became the academic psychology of our day.

The intellectual sources of modern psychology are thus securely anchored in the history of Western philosophy. It is interesting to note, however, that it was at the very moment when Western philosophy was becoming most insecure that psychology began to emerge from her, as colonizers go forth when the mother country grows weak.

There still remained in the background the underlying Platonic point of view, which sought the meaning of life in terms of man's eternal nature. But with the rise of modern rationalistic philosophy, a new conception of man was brought to the fore. The human being was regarded not as a creative spiritual entity but as merely the individual case of impersonal laws that condition his attitudes and determined the patterns of his behavior.

The result was that the theologians bowed out, the philosophers bowed out, and the investigation of the human soul and mind was entrusted to men who worked strictly within a physiologic frame of reference. These men described their researches in a way that sounded most convincing; inevitably so, since they were in harmony with the materialistic spirit of their time. A great wave of optimism accompanied the emergence of psychology as an independent branch of science. From the point of view of nineteenth-century thinking, there could hardly seem to be any more hopeful road to the development of a true psychology, a "science of the soul," than by the laboratory study of animals!

In the period of research that followed, the name "psychology" was retained but the basic content was discarded. What gained acceptance as a new science was, as has often been pointed out, a "psychology without a psyche." This is a point that has been stressed repeatedly over the years both by C. G. Jung and by Otto Rank, and it has been restated recently by a leading academic psychologist, Gordon Allport.[2] The subsequent growth of psychology has thus been based upon a fundamental misnomer, and many confusions and far-reaching errors have been the result. Only in the more recent writings in this field has there appeared, as we shall see later in this book, an attempt to

[2] See Allport's Terry Lectures published under the title, *Becoming Becoming: Basic Considerations for a Psychology of Personality*, New Haven, Yale University Press, 1955.

reconsider and eventually to alter the direction in which psychology is moving in order to come to grips with its original and fundamental subject matter, the *psyche* of man.

The development of psychologic science in its peculiarly modern aspect—constructed, that is, in the image of the natural sciences—took two main forms. One expressed the attitude of the academic researcher seeking to establish a disciplined field of study that would meet the standards of experimental science. The other reflected the practical concern of the physician engaged in the daily task of curing human illness. The first is academic psychology; the second, medical psychology.

The academic approach to psychology concentrated its attention on laboratory work. It investigated the principles of man's personality in terms of the nervous system, the conditioning of the reflexes, the mechanisms by which perception and learning take place, and similar areas in which research could be rigidly defined and limited.

Academic psychology took the lead in eliminating the *psyche* from psychology. Its studies were then intellectually precise, but that was because they baldly omitted the delicate, intangible aspects of man's life which present the greatest problems and the greatest challenge, the difficult questions about himself that man really needs to solve—in short, the reason for studying psychology in the first place. As an eminent academic psychologist, J. A. Gengerelli, recently observed after listing some of the accomplishments of his colleagues, "It seems we are in ignorance of the more important things. . . . Unfortunately, the things we do not know are precisely the things we should know were a science of psychology an accomplished fact rather than a promising program." [3] This, we should note, is precisely the lack that the new depth psychology is capable of filling; and it is here that academic psychology and depth psychology may eventually find their meeting ground.

MEDICAL PSYCHOLOGY AND THE BEGINNINGS OF PSYCHOANALYSIS

In their cloistered position, academic psychologists were free to by-pass those problems that could not be solved with clear experimental proof; but medical psychology could not afford such a luxury. The pressing necessity of bringing relief to suffering human beings made immediate demands. Diagnosis and treatment could not be postponed until ideal conditions of experiment would be available. Medical men interested in psychology were thus impelled to carry out their researches in the best way they could, whether or not statistical controls were possible. The nature of their subject matter prevented their working in laboratories, so they pursued their studies in the public clinics and in their private consultation rooms. Their results were not safeguarded by strict scientific procedures such as the facilities of a laboratory would have made possible; but this lack was more than compensated

[3] *Saturday Review*, March 23, 1957, p. 11.

for by the direct contact with the infinite variety of human conditions and experiences which the physician of the psyche encounters in his daily practice.

The development of medical psychology has thus proceeded in the very midst of the turmoils of modern life. It has, in fact, emerged out of the tensions of existence in an age of mass technology, mass culture, and ideologic uprootedness; for these are the tissues of the illnesses that required psychotherapy and called it forth.

The creative psychiatrists of the nineteenth century were not equipped by training to comprehend the social and historical implications of the situations they were called upon to meet; but they had one great merit that outweighed all their limitations. They faced up to their medical responsibility, accepted the challenge of their times, and where their old techniques were inadequate, undertook to find new ones as best they could to meet their patients' needs. They did not permit themselves to avoid important problems by setting them to one side on the grounds that strict experimental methods could not solve them; but they took account of the seamy side of life which the illnesses of modern personality revealed to them.

In its medical aspect, therefore, psychology became not a cloistered university study, but a science and an art attempting to deal with the actualities of human existence in the modern world. The pioneer psychiatrists of modern times, such men as Kraepelin, Charcot, and Pierre Janet, worked as *physicians of the psyche,* and in that role they penetrated deeply into human nature. With the insights they achieved and the conceptions they developed, they established psychologic practice as a medical discipline upon clinical foundations. Their specific conclusions were far from final, and did not stand the test of time; but their preliminary explorations in the field of psychiatry opened the way for greater pioneers to come.

The first years of the twentieth century began a tremendously productive period in the growth of depth psychology. The generation of psychiatrists preceding Sigmund Freud had gathered considerable clinical material, and their data provided the raw material for Freud's first hypotheses. Even more important than the results of their researches, however, were the methodology and point of view underlying their studies. Working as psychiatrists, they had probed the psychologic forces working below the threshhold of consciousness, and this orientation had great influence in shaping the pattern of Freud's thoughts.

J. M. Charcot, the great French clinician under whom Freud studied in the years immediately preceding his great discoveries, undertook to identify the specific components of pathology in the diseased personality. Freud did not agree with Charcot's conclusions, but he did follow his procedures. In fact, Freud's first epochal insights into those symptoms which earlier theories had ascribed to "hysteria" resulted essentially from the fact that he applied Charcot's method of approach in terms of a sharper, less compromising view of the facts.

After he had worked out his first clinical descriptions and had begun to chart the general outlines of his conception of man, Freud was guided by his fundamental desire to provide a medical frame of reference for diagnosing psychological conditions. The theory of the *unconscious repressed,* which he developed, was a direct attempt to do this, but it was incomplete. In time Freud realized that it was only a first step, and that it required additional conceptions and a larger context. It therefore led eventually —and inevitably, considering the goals of Freud's thinking—to the encompassing view of the structure of the psyche as a whole which took one form in Freud's own work and other forms in the later studies of Adler, Jung, and Rank.

Although the psychiatric investigators of the nineteenth century were very much interested in reaching levels of the personality deeper than conscious awareness, they were for the most part limited by their lack of tools. The practice of hypnosis was of some value, but it still presented many dangers; and at that stage of its development it did not lend itself readily to the probing of the depth levels of personality. At first Freud worked with hypnosis, but he soon concluded that it was an inadequate method for his purposes. He reluctantly set it aside, and it was then, when he was forced to work out new procedures, that he embarked upon the path that eventually led him to his foundational discoveries.

A new study by the hypnotherapist, Milton V. Kline, deals very trenchantly and penetratingly with this question of the reasons for which Freud rejected hypnosis and what the consequences were. The main reason, Kline concludes, was the limited understanding of hypnosis and hypnotic procedures at the time that Freud was carrying on his research. A second factor involved was that Freud believed that a deep hypnotic state would be necessary to permit probing the unconscious to the extent that he desired, whereas it has subsequently been found that a light hypnosis often leads to the most beneficial results in psychotherapy. But, before this could be appreciated, it was necessary to have access to the procedures of therapy that Freud developed only as a result of his rejecting hypnosis. Thus the pertinence of Kline's remark that "Freud's criticism of hypnotic suggestion as therapy was warranted and an abandonment of it in the treatment of the neurosis was a vital factor in developing depth therapeutic techniques." [4]

The great handicap under which Freud's predecessors had worked was that, even though they recognized the importance of the unconscious level of personality, they lacked a reliable means of entering and analyzing it. Freud's great contribution was that he introduced a definite and feasible method of approaching the unconscious and interpreting it. The value of this contribution is quite separate from the question of whether his theories concerning the meaning of the contents of the unconscious are permanently valid. It may indeed be that, compared with the extent of the psyche that depth psychology is finally uncovering, the segment that Freud described is of minor significance. But what is of surpassing importance is that at the point where nineteenth-century psychiatry had reached an impasse, Freud provided new procedures that made it possible to continue the work. Through him, med-

[4] Milton V. Kline, *Freud and Hypnosis*, New York, Julian Press, 1958, p. 17.

ical psychology became fluid again after being bogged down by its own static concepts.

The single factor that contributed most to making this advance possible was Freud's insight into the meaning of dreams. Here again, it was not Freud's specific conclusions that were of primary importance. Time has demonstrated the limitations of Freud's understanding of dreams, his overemphasis on instinctuality and wish fulfillment, and his tendency to rigidify dream symbols. But the mere fact that he demonstrated that dreams are dynamically important in the psyche opened up a whole new avenue of study. Specifically, Freud showed that there are definite psychic processes expressed in the symbolism of dreams, that these processes can be clarified through the interpretation of dream symbols, and that the processes understood by this means are indicative of the structure of the personality as a whole. It hardly mattered at all that the specific theories that Freud proposed for the understanding of dreams reflected an early and incomplete understanding of the subject matter. What was of primary consequence was the fact that the disciplined study of the unconscious had been begun with a strength and insight great enough to command scientific attention. Now others could enter and explore where Freud had broken down the initial barrier. Since he had borne the brunt of introducing major innovations, he inevitably had to pay the penalty of taking the lead. But those who came after him, using the procedures he had developed, were able to move forward and uncover aspects of the unconscious that were not even suspected in Freud's first formulations.

The phrase that came to Freud, "Dreams are the royal road to the unconscious," worked like a magic formula for him, opening up fields of investigation where medical psychology had seemed to have reached a dead end. The realization that dreams provide a means of recapitulating the processes taking place on the deeper levels of the psyche provided a major tool, first of study, then of treatment, and eventually, in the later stage of *holistic* depth psychology of which we shall speak, of individual personality growth toward wholeness. Depth psychology was now in a position to commence a line of work which would eventually enable it to become truly a *depth* psychology, both in theory and practice. Without this means of looking into the unconscious, its development had been seriously restricted; it had had to remain in its medical phase. With it, the scope of study and insight could expand rapidly, and depth psychology soon was led to more than medical vistas.

THE GROWTH OF THE NEW DEPTH PSYCHOLOGY

We can now turn to look more closely at the tremendous wealth of ideas that has grown out of the seeds that Freud planted more than half a century ago. It has been a period of tremendous intellectual fruitfulness, for depth psychology has grown as a living thing. One new tool of study has led to another, a new concept, a new term, a new format of thought, a new perspective. Since Freud, in ways that he could not possibly have imagined and perhaps not even have comprehended, depth psychology has grown by continuous chain reactions leading to unexpected insights and perspectives.

The most effective way to follow the course of this development and to discern clearly the direction in which it is moving is to study the work of the four most fundamental authors in the field, Freud, Alfred Adler, C. G. Jung, and Otto Rank. We find, when we view their total lifeworks together and in historical perspective, that we are dealing not with four separate sets of doctrines but with approximately a dozen that have interpenetrated one another at many points. The work of each divides itself into three and sometimes four periods that are rather sharply marked off by differences in attitude and interest.

In the case of Sigmund Freud, the major biography of Ernest Jones has amply documented the fact that Freud's work must be approached not as a unified body of thought, but as a series of stages of development in which successive changes are involved.[5] A recent study, too, by a historian, Richard Schoenwald, has further dramatized this point;[6] and my own investigations of the personalities and writings of Freud, Adler, Jung, and Otto Rank have indicated that a historical approach to them is essential if we wish to place ourselves in a position where we can under-

[5] Ernest Jones, *The Life and Work of Sigmund Freud*, New York, Basic Books, 3 vols.
[6] *Freud, The Man and His Mind,* New York, Knopf, 1956.

stand the significance of past studies in terms of present needs.[7]

In the case of Freud, we have first the neurologist who was seeking to explain mental illness in terms that would meet the requirements of physical medicine. Then, in the first decades of the century, there was the Freud who was working out his insights into the psychologic nature of dreams and to the processes of the unconscious in general. In the 1920's, there was a Freud growing both disillusioned and wiser, and seeking to extend his conception of depth psychology so that it would be able effectively to go, as he said, beyond the pleasure principle.

He realized that he could not succeed in this, and it was then that he made in the last period of his life a rather fruitless and, one feels, desperate attempt to establish a connection between his lifework and the spiritual roots both of himself and of Western civilization. Freud's publication of his *Moses and Monotheism* was the sign of this. In Freudian terms, Freud's book on Moses was a work of compulsion which revealed his underlying neurosis. But in non-Freudian terms, we can see in his Moses Freud's determined drive toward a personal integrity which he was, unfortunately, not able to achieve.

Correspondingly, we can mark off the various stages in the life and work of Alfred Adler. He began, like Freud, as a medical practitioner, first specializing in diseases of the eye. Perhaps it was this that led him to investigate the differences in the way people see life, that is, the differen-

---

[7] Ira Progoff, *The Death and Rebirth of Psychology*, New York, Julian Press, 1956.

ces in individual psychologic attitudes or, as Adler referred to it, their *styles of life*. He then became interested in studying the effects of physical weaknesses upon the human organism as a whole, and especially in the way these weaknesses are *compensated for* psychologically. It was in the pursuit of this interest that Adler was led to Freud's early hypotheses on the unconscious and that the two became close collaborators.

This period in Adler's life was brief, the period of his close association with Freud, although it was of the greatest importance in his personal development. It was not long before he began to present a point of view that was in marked contrast to Freud's on many points, especially emphasizing the effects of subjective feelings of inferiority upon the personality as a whole. In this period of his work, Adler advocated a method of psychologic therapy that was severely medical in orientation, but when he returned in 1916 from his service in the first World War, he substantially altered his medical emphasis, and switched to a point of view that was much more social and educational in tone. From this, in the later years of his life, Adler moved progressively further toward the frontiers of psychology with a vision of an experience of religious or metaphysical proportions which he hoped would bring the fulfillment of his psychological work. But it must be said that though in his last years Adler envisioned much that is profoundly suggestive, he was able to make only a fraction of it real in practice.

Of all the depth psychologists, the life and writings of C. G. Jung are the most complicated and the most varied.

Jung began, like Freud and Adler, as a medical man. He trained as a psychiatrist, and he devised his famous *Association Tests* shortly before he became acquainted with Freud. When he became identified with the psychoanalytic movement, he soon became Freud's most eloquent spokesman in central Europe; and this lasted until 1912. Then Jung published a book which offered some major additions to Freud's theory of the unconscious, and for the next several years he was engaged in working out the implications of these new conceptions.

In 1921 he published his major work on *Psychological Types,* which contained not merely a descriptive and comparative psychology of individuals, but the basis for an understanding of the underlying process of integration in personality. On the basis of the hypotheses he developed there, Jung became engaged during the 1920's in working out the system of *Analytical Psychology* that eventually became his distinctive trade mark. It was during this decade that Jung received his first major recognition, as it was then generally acknowledged that he had constructed one of the major systems of psychological theory and practice competing with Freud's psychoanalysis within the frame of reference of medical psychology.

Like Adler, however, the achievement of major recognition in the medical field of psychology did not satisfy Jung. He sensed already what Adler too had realized, that the medical field of interest did not encompass all that was at issue in meeting the psychologic problems of modern man. And in the case of Jung, much more than Adler, there was an individual style of temperament passionately curious about religious, philosophic, and mythologic things, wherever the meaning and symbolism of man's destiny were involved.

In the 1930's, Jung invested his energies with ever less reserve and inhibition in exploring the psychologic significance of religious symbolism. The goal was to identify the universal patterns—the archetypes—that underlie the varieties of religious and mythologic symbolism, and to find thereby the nonpersonal dynamic factors that are at work in the deep unconscious levels of the personality. Jung covered a very wide field of research here, ranging from the study of primitive mythology to Tibetan Buddhism, Taoism, Hinduism, Gnosticism, and especially some of the esoteric and heretical Christian cults.

In this regard, Jung has been guided by a very interesting and subtle hypothesis, the significance of which has often been missed. It is his conviction that those religious conceptions and beliefs that have been historically outside the pale of orthodoxy must be accorded a greater importance in studying the psychologic depths of man, because they represent spiritual experiences that have been culturally repressed. On a historical level, therefore, they are in the same relation to the dominantly accepted attitudes as the unconscious is to consciousness in the individual personality. The heretical, the repressed religious beliefs, which often and significantly enough become the orthodoxies of a later era, are especially significant to Jung in the depth study of the modern personality.

It was in the pursuance of this underlying conception that Jung became very deeply involved in the psychologic interpretation of the symbolism and practices of the medieval alchemists. He was subjected to a great deal of attack—even of ridicule—for this, but the several volumes of highly erudite studies of alchemy that he has written significantly enlarged his grasp of psychologic processes. In addition, this work brought Jung into touch with a much larger dimension of psychologic understanding than had been possible for him within the framework of his analytic psychology of psychologic types; but to grasp the value of what he was doing, one has to begin by considering sympathetically, at least for the purpose of study, what Jung was trying to accomplish.

This work on the mysteries of alchemy brought Jung into the middle 1940's, when he was seventy years of age, and what we may speak of as the later and culminating period of his lifework. In this period Jung's work shows two main directions of thought. The first is his attempt to crystallize the observations about the nature of the unconscious that he has accumulated in the course of his psychologic practice. Jung's desire in this regard is to see whether it is possible to develop a conception of the psychic depths that can be integrated into a general theory of the relation of mind and matter. The second direction found in his later work consists in a striving toward a direct experience of those facts in man's life that are usually referred to as "religious." Ultimately, and very profoundly, these two directions in Jung's later work parallel each other, even occasionally touch. But essentially, in the mode of thought and experience that underlies each, they are separate.

The first, we have said, involves Jung's desire to extend and clarify his understanding of the unconscious levels of the psyche. In doing this, he undertakes to draw out some of the implications present in his earlier theory of the unconscious, specifically attempting to relate the theory of the unconscious to the general conception of instincts and patterns of behavior in the human species. Here Jung is very tentatively probing toward an aspect of the human organism that could be understood as being more fundamental than the psychologic on the one hand, and more fundamental than the biologic on the other. It would be a unitary principle underlying psyche and soma and dynamically effective in both.

In pursuit of this, Jung has done some research on the relation between physical events (that is, nonpsychologic events) and events taking place in the psyche, where there seems to be a significant, more than coincidental, correspondence, but where no specific causal factor can be identified. Jung has here attempted to relate psyche and soma in terms of a noncausal principle that he has termed "Synchronicity," and this has involved a very difficult and suggestive work that he has not yet completed either to his own satisfaction or anyone else's.[8] It represents, however, a highly significant enterprise of Jung's later period, and a hypothesis that will surely be explored by future investigators.

[8] See C. G. Jung and W. Pauli, *The Interpretation of Nature and the Psyche,* Bollingen Series LI, New York, Pantheon Books, 1955. Jung's essay in this book, "Synchronicity: An Acausal Connecting Principle," is his main statement on this subject.

Side by side with this, there has been in Jung's later period an attempt to draw from his psychologic researches an awareness, a culminating experience that would express the very essence of his psychologic work with respect to its meaning for him personally and for modern man in general. It involves a nonintellectual, a symbolic experience, an experience of a kind that could be referred to as "metaphysical," dealing with man's ultimate nature and transcending the traditional limits of psychology.

In this connection, Jung wrote what may well be designated as a modern apocalyptic book, *Answer to Job*. Here he sets forth his personal, admittedly subjective experience of the Biblical tradition, centering his attention on the relation between the suffering of Job and the Passion of Jesus. The content and spirit of this book are exceedingly different from Freud's *Moses and Monotheism*, but it is strikingly similar in certain significant personal ways.

It is a book that Jung published, as Freud published his *Moses and Monotheism*, in the grip of compulsion, knowing full well that it would alienate many, even among his close supporters. It is also, like Freud's, a book that can be said, in terms of the older medical psychology, to reveal an underlying neurotic trend in Jung's personality, especially since it expresses a tension in his psyche that intermingles his feelings about his father with his feelings about God. But this psychoanalytic aspect is no more important for understanding Jung than it is for understanding Freud. Much more, what is crucial is the affirmative fact that in his *Answer to Job*, as Freud in his *Moses and Monotheism*, Jung was undertaking a task of personal integrity, seeking to establish for himself his individual connection to the living traditions of Western civilization.

It would seem, if we can judge from Freud's last concerns and from the religious interests of Adler's last years, that to establish in some form such a point of ongoing contact with the traditional past—since that past is experienced as being still psychologically alive in modern man —is somehow a necessity inherent in the study of depth psychology in modern times. And this tells us something about what depth psychology really is, and what it must ultimately do.

There seems to be, underlying the differences in the temperaments and theories of Freud, Adler, and Jung, a common tendency in their work. It is as though the implied goal of depth psychology is to lead to an experience of life that transcends psychology, as its subject matter and orientation have traditionally been defined. And this implication was carried to its logical consequence by Otto Rank, who was the fourth of the classic authors in the history of depth psychology.

Rank was the only one of these four who was not a medical doctor by training, and he was also by some fifteen years the youngest among them. He entered the psychoanalytic movement as a young man shortly after it was founded, and he studied under Freud's direction, eventually to become Freud's main assistant in the study of culture and historical symbolism. The first period in Rank's development, therefore, was completely within the framework of classic, orthodox psychoanalysis. It was during this period that he wrote a major work called *The Myth of the*

Birth of the Hero, in which he undertook to demonstrate the universality of a particular type of myth. It is a book that provides a first bridge between Freud's basic conceptions and the theory of the archetypes that Jung presented a few years later.

Rank worked closely with Freud for almost twenty years. He was, during all this time, a loyal adherent to the psychoanalytic movement. Then in 1924, seeking to extend certain conceptions of Freud, he published a book, *The Trauma of Birth,* which was harshly received and led to his exclusion from the inner circle. Rank seems to have reacted to this with great bitterness and he was deeply, perhaps even lastingly affected by the personal animosities that were characteristic of depth psychology during that period.

The second main stage in his development expressed the negativity of his feelings for he then developed a system, usually referred to as "Will Therapy," which is a suggestive but essentially one-sided reversal of Freud's basic approach. In it, Rank completely discarded the basic conception of the unconscious, and he said that psychology should be concerned only with the conscious will. But at that point, having been personally upset by the treatment he had received from his old friends in the psychoanalytic movement, Rank had rather carelessly and abruptly withdrawn himself from the main stream of depth psychology, and he was not thinking in terms of the unconscious depths at all. Soon, however, he had some second thoughts on the subject, and he reconsidered his position so that, in the next stage of his development, Rank was working once again with the fundamental conceptions of depth psychology.

In this period, which led directly to the insights of his last years that produced Rank's truly creative, lastingly important, and seldom appreciated work, he made use of his background in the cultural sciences to develop an approach to history in terms of the nonrational levels of the psyche. This had a double aspect. On the one hand, it involved an interpretation of history as a whole. On the other hand, and this was really the more important, Rank was studying history in search of clues to the nonrational forces operating in the modern psyche, such as the various kinds of belief in a spiritual reality, the striving for immortality whether through salvation of the soul, through children, or fame, or the production of an enduring work of art; and he especially was interested in the varieties of sexuality in relation to other historic beliefs about the ultimate nature of life.

In doing this, Rank was enlarging upon Freud's basic idea that certain major historical experiences of the human species are deeply engraved in the psyche, and that they are somehow preserved and expressed at various unconscious levels even in the modern person. Rank was also continuing here the search of C. G. Jung for the "archetypes," that is, for the unconscious prototypes of man's conscious actions; and Rank, like Jung, found these in what he called the "mythic stuff" of human existence, the apparently universal themes of man's life that are symbolically expressed in various mythologies, in religious teachings and prophecies, in the modern mind in dreams and fantasies, and in many different kinds of works of art. And Rank was also carrying forward in his historical study Alfred Adler's teleologic conception of the personality, conceiving of man as a unity, an organism who is drawn forward toward a meaning that is inherent in his individual life by dynamic forces that cannot be differentiated as either wholly conscious or wholly unconscious. In this regard, Rank spoke of a "third principle" that is beyond both consciousness and the unconscious, but acts to draw them together, an "integrative will" to life that expresses itself in a variety of cultural forms and permutations in the course of history.

Rank's work thus expresses something of each of the other older authors in depth psychology, and by doing this he indicates the underlying trend of development that takes form in their several works.

The main outcome of Rank's historical study was that it provided him with a large frame of reference within which he could see the emergence of depth psychology in perspective. He could ask then why depth psychology has arisen in modern times, and what is required of it if it would fulfill the historic needs that brought it forth.

Rank's answer to this question is that modern psychology was called forth to fill the vacuum of belief that has appeared in modern times wherever older religious and ideologic beliefs have lost their hold. Psychology was not originally developed consciously as an ideology; but, Rank says, it serves an ideological function. The modern man whose neurosis prevents his living effectively is thereby testifying to the fact that life does not have a livable meaning for him. Psychotherapy is thus called forth in the first place by the failure of traditional values to function; and psychology has a role to play in modern times until the time that some new point of view arises that is capable of providing believable and livable meanings for life. Psychology thus has a transitional function. It has the task of sustaining the modern personality in this interim period when it has lost its old beliefs and has not yet found new ones.)

Now, Rank says, psychoanalysis and each of the other styles of analytic psychology carry out this role simply by providing an intellectual framework—concepts and theories and analytic interpretations that enable the modern man to *feel* that he *understands* his problems. In terms of the particular analytic concepts that he accepts, he can at least feel that he knows where his troubles come from— from his father or his mother, some infantile trauma or inferiority feeling or some difficulty with his psychologic type. Modern man thus derives from analytic psychology a *rationale* for his illness, and this serves, Rank says, as a substitute ideology. But it is a negative ideology because, with its self-conscious, analytic way of reducing every human experience to some small personal event that went before, it is, without realizing it, interpreting its illness in terms of its symptoms, and it thus keeps itself upon a treadmill.

Now, in contrast to this rationalizing ideology of psychoanalysis, Rank holds that modern psychology must take a step that faces up to the ideological role that history has thrust upon it. And it can do this by developing a conception of man drawn in terms of the real possibility of creative experiences in life, of spontaneous and redirective beliefs and actions. With this in mind, Rank called for a step *beyond psychology,* for the phrase *Beyond Psychology* was the title of the culminating book he was engaged in writing when he died.

What Rank meant by this phrase was not by any means an end to psychology as such, but rather the emergence of a new kind of psychology, a psychology that would be aware of its large cultural task, and would turn its main attentions not to the self-conscious analysis of the personal past, but to the development of those psychologic capacities in the human being by means of which new experiences of the meaning of man's existence can be encountered.

In his final judgments about the essence and meaning of modern psychology, Rank crystallized the researches and therapeutic practices of Freud, Adler, and Jung, and of the several phases of the psychoanalytic movement in which he had played a strategic role. His ultimate conclusion expressed an insight that was implicit in the later thinking of the main authors at the point where they faced the consequences of their earlier conceptions. It was the realization that a new kind of psychology is needed, a psychology that is qualitatively different in style and tone, in purpose and in spirit.

The outcome of research in depth psychology during the seminal period of its growth in the first half of the twentieth century has been to show that a new kind of psychology is required. It is a psychology that is capable of transcending itself, and which, eliminating the negative preconcern with the past that is characteristic of the psychoanalytic ideology, opens the way to a direct confrontation with the more than personal, the universal, generic realities of human existence, and the transcendent meanings of life that may be found within man. What is required of depth psychology, then, is that it bring forth a view of the human personality, its nature, and its dynamics, that will make a new, living experience of meaning actually and psychologically possible for modern man. The new style of psychology must be one that gives modern man access to resources that are adequate for a spiritual leap going beyond psychology. And to provide the factual understanding of these resources, together with feasible means of reaching them is the specific purpose of the holistic depth psychology which we shall discuss in later pages.

3 * *The dream of the luminous child*

A MODERN PERSON ADRIFT

Modern man has been described and diagnosed in many different ways. The most impressive and sharply conflicting theories have been used to interpret his troubled life and to weigh his fate on the scales of history. His anxieties have been recorded at great length, analyzed in erudite formulations, and remedies have been prescribed with an air of medical precision. But all this bother has not really been necessary, or would not have been, if man had not lost contact with his basic interior sources of knowledge. For, in the depths of his psyche, the modern person already knows the basis of his difficulties and the road that leads to resolution.

As Alfred Adler once observed, "man knows more than he understands." That is to say, man's faculty for analytic thinking lags behind his capacity for direct intuitive knowledge. Man comprehends directly from within himself the intimate nature of his life, his needs, and his problems, but he loses the thread of his natural wisdom when he turns to concepts and tries to express his knowledge in words.

Man knows more than he understands. That is why the most direct and penetrating insights into the modern situation come not from intellectualizing but from the naïve profundities of the deep psyche. Thus a poet may, upon occasion, send forth a flash of true knowing about man's condition. And sometimes too, a philosopher or a historian in a poetic moment may bring forth a knowing that is more than understanding. When it does happen, it is because the verbalizing intellect has been pressed aside by the force of a new knowledge coming directly out of the depths of man's nature.

This could be spoken of as inspiration from the unconscious. It is composed of the same stuff that dreams are made of, the kind of dreams that naïvely, revealingly, and with more perceptiveness than the conscious mind ever has, set forth the state of affairs in the depths of personality. Such dreams can tell us a great deal about ourselves, and about the human situation in modern times. I would, therefore, like to tell such a dream now, a dream that expresses the deepest needs of a modern woman, and at the same time, with striking simplicity and vividness, reveals an unfulfilled desire that reaches to the core of the modern confusion.

The dreamer was a woman of very moderate education and social background, married, a mother, and employed as a bookkeeper. She had come to talk to me because of an emotional problem that involved her immediate family. She understood the psychological nature of her problem perfectly well; and she realized, at least on a rational level, that it was foolish for her to let it bother her so. But her reasonable attitude did not free her from her trouble, and she remained at the mercy of it in moods that gripped her inexplicably from time to time.

At the beginning of our work together, she told me that she "definitely did not dream"; and when the question of religion was raised, she advised me not to waste time in the future by mentioning that subject again. Religion, she insisted with finality, was a "closed book" for her, and I obligingly dropped the subject. I did not press her for dreams either, but she soon found, nonetheless, that she was aware of having dreams, and her attitude of adamant denial then changed to curiosity mingled with actual interest. At first, when she became aware of dreaming, she could not recall the contents of her dreams at all; only the bare fact of her dreaming remained to her. But after some time she was able to remember her dreams in sufficient detail for us to be able to discuss them together.

As her dreams accumulated, we could discern a process, a pattern of continuity, behind them; and with this we were brought into contact with the deep, unconscious frame of reference, the unrecognized impasses and goals of her life. Finally she had the following dream, which played a major role in the subsequent psychologic transformation that has altered her personality in a fundamental way.

She was strolling in the midst of a large and happy crowd of vacationers on a long pier that stretched far into the water. It was a rather old pier, all of its supports being made of wood. Most of the people were fully dressed, but a few at the further end of the pier were wearing only bathing suits.

Out of the crowd, a man approached the dreamer and showed her a very small, doll-sized baby, about two or three weeks old. The infant was healthy and happy-looking, and the dreamer began to talk to it, play with it, and admire it as one does with a baby, when suddenly the man snatched the baby away and threw it into the water. She was horrified at this, but her feelings changed when she realized that the baby was not drowning, and that it was enjoying itself in the water. The child was not actually swimming, but it had turned onto its back and it was comfortably floating on the top of the water, kicking its feet easily and looking quite content.

Now the dreamer noticed that the infant had an amazing luminosity about it. A shining aura was around it that held the dreamer entranced. She was fascinated by the child, and especially by the glow that emanated from it. Her eyes were as though fastened to the infant and followed its every move intently with an intimate and warm feeling of attachment. As she was speaking of it in telling me the dream, the shape and position of the child's body, together with its wondrous, captivating luminosity, reminded her, she said, of the pictures of the Christ Child on gold-embossed Christmas cards. She had the feeling, she told me—and she said this in a tone of amazement and awe, but also as simply reporting a fact—that this dream seemed to be dealing with something religious or spiritual, much to her surprise.

She said too that now, as she was describing the child to me, the image of it became more vivid than any other dream symbol she had ever seen, and much more vivid and intense than her vision of things in waking life. It became a glowing reality before her mind's eye, and she could perceive its luminous form directly before her as she spoke. This was an experience of a kind she had never had before, neither in quality nor in intensity. The vividness of the image remained with her as a lasting memento of her dream, and it retains the capacity of reawakening her feelings whenever she thinks of it. It has become an actual reality, a fact of her life.

There was then an abrupt change in the action of the dream. The scene remained the same, but the dream seemed to have moved forward in time. She was still standing on the pier, but the infant and the man who had thrown it into the water were gone. Now a young boy of about eleven or twelve years of age came up to her and asked her if she would teach him how to swim. The boy did not resemble anyone she knew in her waking life, but in the dream she had the feeling that his appearance was somehow related to the luminous infant, as though this event represented a further development of that earlier part of the dream.

In answer to the boy's question, she told him to stay in the water and to continue to try to swim. She would stay at the edge of the pier watching him, and if anything went wrong, she would jump in herself and pull him out. She told him that if he stayed in the water he would become accustomed to it, and he would soon gain confidence. Then he would be able to learn to swim by his own experience, and that, she told him, was much the best way.

Now in the dream, as she was talking to the boy, someone came up to her. It may have been her sister or a very old friend, but in any case, it was someone she knew very well; and this person warned her to disappear from view. "You have to hide," she was told. "They're coming for you." There were still many other people enjoying their walk along the pier, but the dreamer was the only one who was being sought and who had to hide. It was only she who did not belong there; only she who had done something that was out of place.

She quickly obeyed the warning to hide, and she did so calmly and methodically, without any feelings of fear or panic. The first thing she did was to hide her wallet. She did this with the greatest care and went to special pains to make sure she found a safe place for it in the wooden props beneath the pier. Then she took off her clothes, leaving herself in her bathing suit, and she hid them in a second place under the pier, but with somewhat less care than she had hidden the wallet. Finally, she hid herself in the water under the pier, and there she waited until the danger would be passed.

Soon, looking up to the pier above her, she saw two men walking among the crowd looking for her. She saw their faces in the dream and they were complete strangers to her. One was bald and the other was swarthy, but there was nothing at all sinister about them. They looked like two businessmen or government officials, and they did not seem to be searching for her with great determination. They simply asked some people if they had seen her, looked for her among the faces of the crowd, and then they left. As she hid in the water observing them, it was, the dreamer told me, "like watching a movie to see them." But now they were gone, and the way was clear for her to return to the surface.

There were several additional scenes in this dream, for it was an unusually long one, and one that was very well remembered in its details. These additional phases of the dream referred to later periods in the dreamer's life, to future stages in the development of her personality that were still only possibilities. The dream, however, brought all of these together into a single experience, for the nature of dreaming is to express the wholeness of the personality in a way that transcends time, drawing past, present, and future into the unity of a single moment.

In its latter portions, the dream appeared to be describing potentialities of growth and fulfillment which it, on the depth level of the psyche, already accepted as real, but which, in actuality, would only become real after the first part of the dream had been lived through and experienced with all its implications in the affairs of life. We had to turn our attention to first things first, and thus it was the earlier portions of the dream which we have described that became the center of study in our work; for it was this that provided the key both to her basic inner need and the resolution of her problem.

The most striking characteristic of the first parts of the dream, from the point of view of the dreamer, was the vividness and intensity with which it forced itself upon her. Previously she had maintained that she hardly ever dreamt at all, and that whatever she did dream was of no significance. But this dream was clearly a fact. It really could not be denied, and what made the deepest impression upon her was her realization that she had not created the dream. It had come into being by itself, uninvited and unaided. She had not thought it up with her mind, nor had she invented it with her imagination. It was indeed *her* dream, but she herself had not created it. It had arisen, rather, from a source of its own, a source that was in some way independent of her and also within her.

The fundamental feeling that she experienced as she came to tell me the dream was awe before the forces that had made the dream. Here was evidence of something at work, something mysterious in its origins and dark in its meaning, something capable of making great events take place within her without either her knowledge or her consent. Not only by the dream's vivid and shaking clarity, but by the strength of its impact upon her whole emotional being, she felt compelled now to pay attention to it and to inquire seriously and sincerely what its meaning for her life might be.

THE REPRESSION OF SPIRIT AND ITS AFFIRMATION

We proceeded slowly and carefully in our efforts to discover what the dream was trying to say. What feelings did the dreamer have about the luminous child in the water? "It's like a child I've missed," she answered. Did it represent an actual physical child? No, she had already borne children, she said, and she had no desire for another. Her feeling was that what was being represented was more like a spiritual child. It was something of a spiritual nature that wanted to come to birth in her.

Only at that point did she tell me something she had suppressed in all our previous meetings. She had once, indeed, been interested in religion, but she had not been able to find a satisfying experience. She had not even been able to find anyone with whom she could talk through her religious problems. That was why she had closed the books where religion was concerned, and at the time she had been completely convinced that she would never open them again. Now she was beginning to wonder.

She told me then that she had been born a Lutheran, but seeking a more intense religious contact, she had converted to Catholicism in her late teens. Here, however, she had been disappointed, for the kind of feeling she had sought did not happen to her. She remained within the Church, married in it and brought her children up within it, but she herself lost her interest in Catholicism so that her interest and her church attendance dwindled.

For some time, however, she continued to feel a general religious interest. She thought she might be able to find an answer outside the Church, but she had not searched very hard and so she had not found a satisfying channel. Also, her family atmosphere was not favorable, for when she spoke to her relatives or to close friends about her desires in this direction, they laughed at her and told her to "go bang a drum in the Salvation Army." She found this ridicule particularly painful to endure and eventually abandoned her search, repressing her religious feelings because, she thought, they could not possibly ever be fulfilled. And worse than that, the teasing of her friends made her feel that there was "something odd" about her for thinking of religious questions, and thus with special effort she deliberately repressed these thoughts. She wanted to be "normal" enough to be able to retain her friends and to hold her job as a bookkeeper.

With this new information, the meaning of the dream began to open to us. The luminous child was indeed a religious symbol for her, and also a symbol of something young and new entering her life, something undeveloped, holding great attraction for her and yet just beyond her reach.

There had been something like that earlier in her life. She had felt the first stirrings of spiritual desires, but before she could come to know it well, it had been taken away from her. The glowing quality of the child signified the sense of the divine which, the dream indicated, was still present in her unconscious. It had been taken away from her. It was thrown into the water out of her reach, but she still felt drawn to it. Its luminous, transcendent quality was still real for her. Her unconscious perceived the divine, angelic glow of the spiritual child, and she was altogether fascinated by it. The first scene in the dream suggested, therefore, that the religious desire that had been unsatisfied before was still present in her. The dream said that although it was out of her reach, it was important that she pay attention to it.

The incident of the luminous child also presented a question. When the child was taken away from her, and thrown into the water, would it be destroyed? In the dream her first feeling about this was horror, for she thought the child would surely drown. She felt, in other words, that the possibilities of spiritual growth in her would be destroyed. But then came the realization in the dream that had particular meaning in her immediate situation. The child still lived. The possibility of new life development was still present for her. She was drawn to it; she was to pay attention to it. The question then—and this was the central concern of the dream—was how this new spiritual being was to grow into her life.

The answer that the dream gave was in terms of process, of gradual and continuing development. Thus in the next scene of the dream the child does not appear, but there is instead a young boy, who represents a further but still early stage in her development. In later portions of the dream, there were still further expressions of progressive growth, eventually reaching a mature man and then a minister who plays a saving role at a culminating point in the dream.

The young boy had come to learn. How was he to swim, that is, how was he to move about in the waters of life and of the spirit? The feeling in the dream was that the young boy was somehow connected with the luminous child as though he represented a further stage in the growth of the new spiritual being. But there was still a lack of knowledge. The question of how to swim means how can the spirit in her, which has grown from a babe to a young boy, learn to maintain itself in life? It is her own life problem, her problem of growth.

What is of great significance in the dream is that the boy came to her for instruction as to how to swim. The feeling of the dream was that somehow she already possessed the necessary knowledge. She had it within herself. Therefore the advice that she was able to give the boy was encouragement. Go ahead, try, she said to the young man, even assuring him that if any difficulty arose, she herself would be there to help him. This was a major expression of an inner confidence, for here she was expressing her unconscious sense of contact with the sustaining and creative forces of life. In the process of the development of the spirit she had no fear. From within her own self, and without consciously understanding the reason, she was secure in her feeling that she would know what to do at crucial points in her new education in life.

It was at this point that the interruption came in her

dream. Someone was coming to look for her, and she had to hide. Up to that point her development had been progressing well. But now there was uncertainty and the "authorities" seemed to feel that she should not be paying attention to the development of her spirit. Thus the woman who told her to hide was either her sister or a close friend, someone representing those intimate friends whose ridicule had caused her to drop her interest in religious things in earlier years. It was the same kind of situation. She had been turning her attention to the development of the spirit in herself, and once again it was the people in her immediate social environment who wanted her to desist.

The next scene in the dream provided the key to this. When she hid from the men who were coming for her, she hid first her wallet, then her clothes, and finally herself; but in the dream the wallet seemed to have by far the greater importance. I asked her what seemed to make the wallet so important in the dream. Was there much money in it? Oh no, she said; but there was a card in it, a card of identification. If they found the wallet with the card in it, they would know *who she truly was* and then they would know that she did not belong with them.

It was not difficult to understand this part of the dream in the light of the frustrations in religious experience she had told me about. The luminous child and the young boy in the dream were signs that her spiritual desires were becoming active once again, and this time were starting to grow. But again her self-consciousness before the ridicule of friends who gave the spiritual no place in life was arising to inhibit her. They would say she was a fool to be concerned about such things, that she was a "little odd." If she could hide it they would never know about her private desire. But if they found the card of identification, they would know about her true interest, and then she would be an outcast among them. This would mark her off as different; she would no longer belong.

With a dream speaking as strongly as this one, and especially since this dream came with sufficient intensity to convince the dreamer of the reality of the processes of the deep unconscious, there was not much difficulty in understanding it, and in integrating it into the ongoing life experience of the dreamer. The dream carried its own clear way of interpretation, once the road to it had been opened.

To open this road, all that was necessary was to realize that the spiritual side of the personality need not be repressed. It is not a sign of foolishness, nor of neurosis. It is not something to be diagnosed, and not something to be hidden. And the fact that family and friends may raise an eyebrow at any spiritual interest that goes beyond the simple conventional forms must be understood as a reflection of the temper of thinking in modern times.

The emphasis on material success and on tangible, secular standards of consumption has caused the interest in the spirit to drop to a low degree. What is repressed in modern times is much less sexuality than spirituality. The person who suffers most because of this is the one who feels the urge to religious expression and inner spiritual development, and yet cannot bear the social pressure that ridicules anything that varies from the materialist view of life, or from the conventional ritual observances of religion. Such persons suffer because something deep in their natures, something they urgently need to express and develop, is forced to be repressed. And for such people, the suppression of the spiritual can frequently have its outcome in neurotic symptoms.

In the case of our dreamer, the first effect of her understanding of her dream was that she was able to accept the spiritual side of life. This meant that she could accept herself, and much more, from the impact and inner conviction of the dream, she realized that there is a source of insight and self-direction within her that provides her with the capacity to emerge whole from her difficulties. Knowing this, she could not only accept herself, but she could trust herself. She could have confidence in the unconscious forces working within her, helping her, indeed forcing her under pain of neurosis to find her true deep self.

Our work together could then go in another direction. Having accepted herself and affirming the powers of her deep psyche, the next task was to reach further into the resources of her unconscious, to draw forth what was latent and potential there, and to assist it in coming to expression. For this we used another kind of technique that the new depth psychology provides.

The dream of the luminous child was a personal dream involving the needs and repressions of a single individual. It was, however, symptomatic of the situation of many persons living in the midst of the intellectual and spiritual transformations of modern civilization. Something in man calls out for spiritual contact and for the inner meaningful development of his life. In past times and cultures, this has taken the form of a great diversity of religions and sects, faiths and superstitions. In recent generations of the modern age, the rationalistic view of life and the empiric tests of science have weakened these old doctrines by placing them beyond intellectual acceptance, and it has swept many of them away altogether.

Nonetheless, though the specific beliefs may not pass muster when scanned by the dry light of scientific understanding, the basic quality in the human person that originally called them forth is still there. The need remains, and it is much more than a need. Many of those who are strongly committed to the rigorous methods of science have felt that there is something essential in the nature and meaning of man's life that is far more fundamental and important than the forms and even the specific content of the religious doctrines he has held in the past. It is as a seed of spiritual striving in man, a seed that is not weakened by science as perhaps some of the old faiths are, but is rather reinforced by science, and so calls upon the resources of science to assist it in its continuing quest.

Many persons devoted to science have felt a conflict within themselves similar to that of the dreamer of whom we have spoken. They too have a luminous child in the depths of their being, a spiritual desire for meaning in life which has been from the beginning the deep unconscious drive motivating their striving for truth through science. And they, too, in the face of the narrowed view of science in a materialistic technicians' society, have repressed their feeling for the spirit lest, like our dreamer, they be thought "a little odd."

So basic a reality in man cannot, however, stay buried for long. It has forced itself to the surface in the writings of a number of scientists in fields that range from physics and mathematics to biology and the study of history. The inner experiences of these men as well as the objective results of their investigations are of considerable significance for the understanding of modern man and for an appreciation of the creative role depth psychology can play in his life. Especially meaningful in this regard is the life and work of the scientist/statesman Jan Christian Smuts, to whom we now turn. He lived on the borderland that connects science with the spirit, and his attempt to elucidate the underlying unity he perceived there carries many useful lessons.

4 * *A prototype of modern man: the life and thought of Jan Christian Smuts*

THE PLACE OF PERSONALITY IN EVOLUTION

For an individual to be called a *modern man* signifies something more than the mere fact that he happened to be born at a date that left him no alternative but to live out his years in the vicinity of the twentieth century. It means something more also than a person who has uncritically absorbed the fads and foibles of his generation. Rather, to be called a *modern man* in a full and meaningful sense implies that a person has felt in the depths of his being the impact of the basic and characteristic problems of the modern age. And more, it means that he has not run away from these problems, but has permitted them to work within him, to disturb him profoundly and intimately, and that in opening himself to experience their meaning, he has drawn them toward a resolution, at least within his own understanding.

One of the most fundamental problems of this kind concerns the difficulties that arise from the modern way of thinking about man as a member of the animal kingdom. Since ancient times, there have been many conceptions of human nature phrased in materialistic terms, understanding man as exclusively a creation of the natural world. But the Darwinian view that the evolution of species takes place by means of natural selection carried all previous materialisms to a new level. It presented a specific and documented principle to account for the connection between animal species and the human species. Its impact was much greater than any ordinary scientific hypothesis, for it was indeed much more than a hypothesis. It was a view of life, an encompassing conception of the life process as a whole, and of man's place within it.

The Darwinian theory of evolution brought to modern civilization a full perspective in which all forms of life, vegetable and animal, could be understood, human beings among them. After Darwin, any person who gave even the slightest lip service to the spirit of science had to retain a primary place in his thinking for the conception that man is not only a part of nature, but that he has emerged in the course of time out of the animal kingdom. What then, was he to conclude about the creative element in human personality, and about what had been spoken of as the *spiritual* in man?

This question loomed large in the mind of many sensitive individuals living in the latter part of the nineteenth century. And one of the most significant of these persons, in terms of the range of his knowledge and public activities and the depth and drive of his understanding, was the great South African political leader, military strategist, and philosopher, Field Marshal Jan Christian Smuts.

Smuts was born in 1870 in South Africa of Dutch background. He studied law at Cambridge and there, following the extralegal bent of his mind, wrote a penetrating study of Walt Whitman subtitled significantly, "A Study in the Evolution of Personality." Written at the age of twenty-five, this work was never published; but it was in many ways prophetic in its insights with respect both to Smuts's personal growth and the eventual emergence of a new psychology capable of understanding the *whole* personality in depth.

After Cambridge, Smuts returned to South Africa to practice law, and there he soon became active in political life. He played a leading role in the Boer War, and though he was barely thirty years of age, he became a senior general on the Boer side. He fought the British stubbornly, and then concluded a generous and friendly peace that made it possible for South Africa to maintain a strong position within the British Commonwealth.

In 1907, as Minister of Interior in the South African government, it was Smuts's task to oppose Mahatma Gandhi, who was then a young lawyer leading the Indians in South Africa in an early, premature version of his Satyagraha. This was a great struggle of iron wills in which, as it was wryly said at the time, if the conferences lasted long, it was because the two political leaders were talking philosophy. Smuts seems to have been the victor in this struggle on the political level, but spiritually, Gandhi had a great and lasting influence upon him. The two men were able to meet on the most cordial terms later on, sharing their understanding of the depth levels on which history moves.

In the first World War, Smuts served as a general in the Allied armies, and he held major positions in the British War Cabinet. His position was prominent at the Versailles peace conference, and he was probably the closest collaborator and strongest international supporter of Woodrow Wilson's program for the League of Nations. After the war, he was Prime Minister in South Africa until 1924, when he suffered a stinging reverse at the polls. At first, Smuts interpreted his defeat as a personal rejection by his countrymen; but he soon saw the constructive side of it. Then he seized upon his political disaster as an opportunity to work out his philosophical reflections on the nature of the human personality and man's place in biological evolution. These conceptions had been maturing in him for twenty years, ever since his early work on Whitman. Now they were expressed in a major work, *Holism and Evolution,* which took the Darwinian conception of evolution as its starting point, and undertook to show how human personality emerges from this natural process with the creative faculties of mind and spirit.

Smuts was accorded many honors for this work of scholarship. He was named president of the British Society for the Advancement of Science, and eventually Chancellor of Cambridge University. When the second World War came, he played a major role again as a general in the Allied armies, rising this time to the rank of Field Marshal. At the peace he had an opportunity to further the idealism he had originally shared with Wilson in founding the League of Nations. He visited America for a brief and fruitful contact with President Roosevelt, and played a major role in the founding of the United Nations. The postwar years, however, left him much to lament. In addition to the shadows that he perceived upon the international scene, he was once again defeated in the South African elections, and the efforts he had made toward the establishment of a liberal culture in South Africa were washed away in the floodtide of racialism under which the country is still submerged. He died in 1950.

Our interest in Jan Christian Smuts here, however, is not in his political activities, nor is it in his personal achievements as an individual. What is significant for us, rather, is the development of his thought, the conception of man in relation to nature, which he felt as so important a part of his life that he worked on it in the midst of all his political and military ventures from the time of his first research into the development of personality in Whitman.

Smuts's life stands out as being the most complete instance of a truly *modern man,* understanding by that term a person who has lived closely in touch with his times, has felt the impact of its problems, and has undertaken to resolve them both within himself and in his activities in the world. Smuts's life was a wonderful expression of this, because of the range of his involvement in contemporary affairs—from warfare and peace conferences to politics, philosophy of science, and the chancellorship of a major university—and especially because of his high degree of sensitivity to the specifically *human* needs of modern times.

The core of Smuts's personal quest for understanding concerned the problem we have mentioned as the starting point of modern thinking: How it is possible that man derives from the animal kingdom, and yet is inherently a creative, spiritual being? Smuts was not interested in this as a merely intellectual question separated from life. It was a matter of necessity, of deep personal concern. For him the purpose of the knowledge he sought, no matter how abstract it turned out to be, was specifically to resolve his questions as a human being living in modern times, and especially to assist himself in growing as a person.

While he was still a law student at Cambridge, Smuts became engaged in the line of investigation that was to culminate in his major book, *Holism and Evolution*. It was as though, even in those early days, Smuts was already anticipating the needs of the creative growth that was to be the continuing principle of his mature life. He was, in fact, searching out the principles that would make it a practical possibility. Thus, in Cambridge, the direction of his inquiry led him to investigate human personality, to see how it unfolds and matures in the world of nature, and to find its ultimate meaning and potentialities.

The reason that Smuts as a young man was anxious to discover the principles of personality growth was in order to make use of these principles himself in developing his own personality. He understood by *personality* not a superficial façade of sociality that would help him "influence people" and achieve worldly success, but the inner capacities latent in the nature of personality as a creative entity in itself. He was interested in coming into contact with the essential core of being in man, believing that to develop this would bring to realization the fullest extent of what is potential in man. As a young man, Smuts had had an inner vision of this as a possibility for his own life, and while he was a law student at Cambridge he undertook to discover by empirical research what the principles involved in it were, in order to practice them.

It is very useful for our understanding of modern thought to observe how Smuts went about his search. If he had lived in a premodern period of history, he would very probably have approached his question in terms of God and the divine as the creative principle in man. But since Smuts was born toward the close of the nineteenth century, after Darwin, he could not take traditional religious conceptions as his starting point. He could only begin with the view that man is a part of nature and then undertake to find, in the structure of man as an animal species, those qualities that eventually emerge as that intangible creative factor that Smuts called *personality*.

Starting with this general view, he needed specific case material. He could possibly have undertaken a broad comparative study of a large number of individuals who had reached a high degree in the development of personality. But he did not want to get involved in a cumbersome work of scholarship that might divert him from his immediate goal of personal understanding. Smuts decided that the best, most empirical, and most instructive mode of procedure for him was to choose a single individual who had attained a high level of personality, a modern person if possible about whom sufficient information was available, and to study that individual closely. The best case would be one who had left a written record describing his experiences articulately and in detail, for then there would be objective material that could readily be analyzed and interpreted.

The life and writings of Walt Whitman admirably suited his purpose. Whitman's work might not be universally accepted as superior poetry—and, in fact, in Smuts's day Whitman was far out of favor in the literary circles both of England and South Africa—but the nature of his spiritual experience and perception and the quality of his personality exemplified the principle of personality that Smuts was trying to understand and to make real in himself.

He found a kindred spirit in Whitman, one who had touched the profound unity of life and had merged with it in the depths of his being. But Whitman, as an individual, was only the special case of a general principle that might be found to be operative throughout the process of natural evolution and in the human species in particular.

With the material he drew from his study of Whitman, Smuts was able to validate and amplify this conception.

Whitman's poems contained a very strong sense of continuity within the life process as a whole. Sometimes this was expressed in a casual, almost monotonous listing of things and places, a seeming catalogue of creation, and many readers did not see the point. At other times, Whitman would speak of past and future, of foreign races and climes, with an intense intimacy of feeling that would imply that he was somehow personally participating in each of these strange and varied things and places and people.

In the first aspect of cataloguing, Whitman would seem cold and objective to his readers. In the second aspect, he would seem naïvely romantic and subjective. But Smuts saw through the masks of communication in Whitman's poems to the core of the experience of nature extending through time, reaching from far in the past, through the present, into an open future. Smuts knew what Whitman knew, that the individual Personality is the aperture of time, the eye of the needle through which all creation must pass in its movement onward.

He perceived, therefore, that the objectivity of description and the subjectivity of personal identification in Whitman's poems were two sides of a single coin. All the creations of the past have their meaning in the individual personality who experiences their reality in the present moment and who thus transports them to the future. All of creation leads to the individual person, and he in turn has always been present in creation through all past ages. Thus the processes of natural evolution are not foreign to us as individual human persons, for we have ever been part of it; it has all been moving to the point where we now are, and it continues through us now as we feel it, and participate in it, and move forward with it.

It was in such a sense that Smuts interpreted the following passages from Whitman:

I am an acme of things accomplished
And I am an enclosure of things to be.
My feet strike an apex of the apices of the stairs.
On every step bunches of ages, and larger bunches between each step,
All duly travelled, and still I mount and mount.

Rise after rise bow the phantoms behind me,
Afar down I see the huge first Nothing, I knew I was even there,
I waited unseen and always, and slept through the lethargic mist,
And took my time, and took no hurt from the foetid carbon—.

Smuts perceived the inner side of these lines, and so he spoke of Whitman's writing as "a matchless account of human evolution." [1] Not everyone, perhaps, would read such passages in the same way, and it is therefore interesting to note that Smuts's opinion has recently been echoed by another authority on Darwinian evolution, the eminent biologist, Julian Huxley. In his *Evolution in Action*,

[1] Quoted from Sarah Gertrude Millin, *General Smuts*, Boston, Little, Brown, 1936, Vol. I, pp. 43, 44.

Huxley wrote in 1953: "I can think of no other saying more pregnantly apt to this last chapter of mine (on the human phase of evolution) than this of Walt Whitman's in his 'Song of the Open Road'; 'All part away for the progress of souls . . . Of the progress of the souls of men and women along the grand roads of the Universe, all other progress is the needed emblem and sustenance.' It is couched in evolutionary terms; it is based on the postulate of progress; it brings out the value of symbols in supporting human effort; and above all it sets forth the soul, which in this context is to be equated with the individual personality at its highest and fullest, as the ultimate standard by which we must judge all other human achievements." [2]

Whitman perceived that human personality is the core and meaning of evolution because he had reached a stage in his inner development that enabled him to recognize, and spiritually participate in, the holistic process of the cosmos. Whitman had reached that high plateau of holistic personality, and his poetry was the outer embodiment of this inner achievement. It was this in Whitman that Smuts appreciated and with which he felt a kinship. It was because of this achievement of personality that he wished to study Whitman, to gain information he could use in his wn personality growth. He found it in lines like these:

I will not make poems with reference to parts,
But I will make poems, songs, thoughts with reference to Ensemble,

[2] Julian Huxley, *Evolution in Action.* Mentor reprint p. 118.

And I will not sing with reference to a day, but with reference to all days,
And I will not make a poem nor the least part of a poem
but has reference to the soul,
Because having looked at the objects of the Universe,
I find there is no one nor any particle of one but has reference to the soul.

The wholeness of creation, the fullness of evolution, find
meaning and fulfillment in the individual human personality. This was the lesson that Smuts drew from Whitman's
experience, and he carried it further into a larger, more
comprehensive formulation concerning the nature of evolution in general. He had written his Whitman manuscript in 1895. In 1910 he made an attempt at expressing
the larger theory in a manuscript entitled "An Inquiry
into the Whole"; but this also was never published. Only
in 1924, when he suffered his major setback at the polls,
did he have an opportunity to work out his holistic conception of evolution in its full scope. This was published in
1926 as *Holism and Evolution*.

In *Holism and Evolution,* Smuts presented his theory
that natural evolution is a continuous process moving
toward ever more developed "wholes." And what are
wholes? "Every organism, every plant or animal, is a
whole," Smuts answers, "with a certain internal organization and a measure of self-direction, and an individual
specific character of its own." "What is not generally
recognized," he adds, "is that the conception of wholes

covers a much wider field than that of life, that its beginnings are traceable already in the inorganic order of Nature. . . ." "In the view here presented," Smuts writes, "*wholes* are basic to the character of the universe, and Holism, as the operative factor in the evolution of wholes, is the ultimate principle of the universe." [3]

In beginning his study of Whitman, Smuts had set his goal as an empiric understanding of the highly developed holistic personality, as exemplified in Whitman. As a result of that study, however, he came to the realization "that Personality was only a special case of a much more universal phenomenon, namely, the existence of wholes and the tendency towards wholes and wholeness in nature." [4] Now, in his *Holism and Evolution,* he was setting out to demonstrate what the "universal phenomenon" involved. He wanted to show "that this whole-making or holistic tendency is fundamental in nature, that it has a well-marked ascertainable character, and that Evolution is nothing but the gradual development and stratification of progressive series of wholes, stretching from the inorganic beginnings to the highest levels of spiritual creation." [5]

Smuts presented a schematic outline of that Holistic conception of evolution but in later years, looking back at it objectively, he had to concede that it had been considerably lacking in supportive data on the side of biology.

[3] Jan Christian Smuts, *Holism and Evolution,* New York, Macmillan, 1926, pp. 98, 99.
[4] *Ibid.,* p. vi.
[5] *Ibid.,* p. v.

Not that that data might not be found—indeed, as we shall see when we discuss the work of Edmund Sinnott, it is ready at hand—but Smuts was not by training in a position to marshal the factual material needed at the time. Looking back at the book and its significance, Smuts made, however, a correct judgment in saying that what was really important in his book was not the details of factual information, but the general hypothesis of Holism, which is on the one hand a theory of evolution and on the other hand a conception of man and of life, a *Weltanschauung* in terms of which the personality of modern individuals may be led to higher stages of development.

Thus, Smuts wrote in judging the nature and significance of his book, "The principle is stronger than the supporting argument and is in a sense not dependent on it. At its lowest level, the argument may be looked upon as in the nature of illustrations and exemplifications, rather than as actual proof of the principle of Holism. That principle is that reality is fundamentally holistic, and that all the patterns of existence in which it finds expression tend to be wholes, or holistic in one degree or another. The book traces the evolution of these wholes in the physical and biological domains, and tries to show that new, more complex wholes arise on the basis of older, simpler, perhaps more settled and stable wholes by a process of *emergence*. The new whole incorporates older wholes as material, but is essentially new and transcends the material or parts on which it is based. The reality is in the new whole thus emerging, and not in the sum of the parts from which it has emerged. This process of whole-making con-

stitutes evolution, and makes the world a progressive series of wholes or individual patterns, from its physical beginnings, in matter or energy, to the flowering out of life
in all manifold forms and grades." [6]

TOWARD HOLISTIC GROWTH

The large schematic conception of evolution which we
have been describing here came into being as a result of
one main motivation. This was the search of Jan Christian
Smuts as a young man for a frame of reference in which to
see the meaningfulness of his life, and for a knowledge
that would enable him to develop the creative capacities
he felt awakening as potentialities within him.

With these purposes, it was essentially a psychological
knowledge that Smuts required. But when in the 1890's as
a student at Cambridge he looked to the young science of
psychology for assistance, he found nothing that seemed
even to relate to his problem. Although it was an inherently psychologic question that he was raising, the psychology of his day was not in a position to make any significant
contribution to an answer. It was of no help to him, but
where else could he turn?

There were two main alternatives. One was traditional
religion; the other was science. Smuts, as a *modern man* in
the sense that we have defined that phrase, had little alter-

[6] *The Thoughts of General Smuts,* compiled by his private secretary, P. B.
Blankenberg, Cape Town and Johannesburg, Juta & Co., Ltd., 1951, p. 161.

native here. Although he felt a strong sensitivity to spiritual things, traditional religion could not contain him, for the attitude of scientific research had left an indelible imprint upon him. When he asked his central questions, what the nature of man is and what the principles of personality growth are, he could not be satisfied with theological answers. The only kinds of answers that could now seem adequate to him after the impact of the scientific way of thinking were those that interpreted man within an evolutionary perspective of natural process.

There were thus two main factors at work in the background of Smuts's thinking. One was his strong desire for knowledge of a kind that would assist his personal growth. The other called for strict adherence to the scientific point of view, especially with respect to understanding the biological nature of man. And these two divergent tendencies of thought, which constitute one of the central conflicts in the modern mind, found a means of being reconciled, at least within Smuts as an individual. Smuts integrated them by drawing from the study of natural evolution insights that led directly to the kind of psychological knowledge he required.

Smuts developed his interpretation of evolution, calling attention to the fact that the tendency to form new wholes —ever more advanced unities—is a main characteristic of the evolutionary process. Further than this, he pointed out, a special case of the tendency toward the formation of wholes is the emergence of human personality out of the evolution of animal forms. Personality represents the highest point of development, the most advanced whole, to be produced by the process of natural evolution.

This line of thinking took Smuts up to the point where he could begin to approach the question that was the real reason for his search. Personality has emerged in the course of evolution, and it is the distinctive characteristic of the human species. It is the special sign of the *wholeness* of the human being. Yet there are apparently many different gradations in the quality of personality that can be developed in specific individuals within the human species. Personality is a tremendous potentiality in man, but there is very wide variation in the degree to which its promise, present innately in man as Homo sapiens, is fulfilled. This brought Smuts to the question to which all his study of evolution had been leading: what principles and techniques are there for drawing forth the largest possible development of the personality potential in man?

This was a question that could best be approached in a scientific spirit. Smuts did so from the very beginning, even before he had worked out his holistic interpretation of the evolutionary process. He hit upon the empiric procedure of studying each individual case of highly developed personality in order to draw inferences and general conclusions as to the dynamic principles at work in advanced personality growth. As we have indicated, his study of the life and work of Walt Whitman as an instance of "the evolution of personality" was his pilot study in this regard, a test case of his holistic conception.

Later, in writing his *Holism and Evolution,* Smuts set

forth some of the frame of reference that was in the background of the kind of inquiry that his study of Walt Whitman exemplified. He looked at the psychological work being done at that time (which by 1925, when *Holism and
Evolution* was completed, already included a substantial
development of Freudian psychoanalysis and several of
the main schools of thought within depth psychology) and
he asked how they contributed to the question that
seemed of basic importance to him: namely, what principles and procedures are involved in the development of
personality?

The main core of academic psychology, what Smuts referred to as "pure psychology," offered no approach at all
to the creative dynamics of personality. "Take for instance," Smuts wrote, "Professor James Ward's *Psychological Principles,* which is not only a standard work, but
embodies and expands what has become the great classic in
psychology in the English language. It consists of eighteen
chapters, the first four of which are devoted to a general
analysis and description of mental functions, while the
main body of the work, consisting of twelve chapters, contains a detailed discussion of the various forms of mental
activity, such as sensation, perception, imagination, mem-
ory, feeling, emotion, and action, intellection, forms of
synthesis in the judgment, intuition, and the categories,
belief and the elements of conduct. The last two chapters
only are devoted to the concrete individual and character-
ology, and form merely a distant approach to the subject
of Personality." [7]

[7] Smuts, *Holism and Evolution,* pp. 280-281.

Ward's book, published in 1918, but said by Ward to have been forty years in the writing, was indeed representative of the style and tone of academic psychology up to the early years of the twentieth century. He was a professor of psychology and philosophy at Cambridge, where Smuts perhaps came into contact with him.[8] His work was a clear example of the fact that psychological theory at that time had hardly begun to free itself from the habits of thinking that lingered on from its earlier connection with epistemologic philosophy. It was still so enmeshed in intellectualism that, as Smuts remarked, "even the mental side of Personality fails to be properly explored and understood." [9]

Since that time, much has been added in academic psychology, especially in the field of personality theory. These additions, however, have come mainly as a result of the pioneering of Freud and his successors in the study of the unconscious.

The impact of depth psychology upon academic psychology brought the twentieth-century study of man much closer to satisfying the criteria Smuts set for it. He still had, however, a serious criticism to make. The psychoanalytic conception of man involved a basic dichotomy in the personality, a division between consciousness and the unconscious. It is true that this distinction has always been made in theoretical terms with the clear proviso that the reader keep in mind that it is a purely hypothetical divi-

---

[8] See Edwin G. Boring, *A History of Experimental Psychology*, New York, Appleton Century Co., 1929, pp. 453, 456, 457.
[9] *Holism and Evolution*, p. 279.

sion marked off for purposes of study within the unity of the personality. Both Freud and Jung have been explicit in this regard, emphasizing that they had no intention of hypostasizing the unconscious and making a *thing* of it artificially. Smuts, however, had a criticism that cut beneath the entire conception of the unconscious, a criticism that was all the more significant because he made it in full recognition of the importance of understanding the depth levels of personality.

Smuts took the view that the very act of separating consciousness from the unconscious falsified the nature of personality. It breaks into segments what is essentially unitary, and by doing this it gives an inherently untrue picture of the way human personality lives and grows. Analysis falsifies the essential inner integrative process of personality; and the reason for this is, as Smuts stated it in his study of Whitman, that there is an "ultimate internal unity that shapes the innumerable products of life into an orderly and harmonious whole." [10]

The development of personality is to be understood, in other words, not in terms of the conflict or balancing of separate segments within the individual, but in terms of a single dynamic principle present in the seed of the organism, and working toward unfoldment. This is a single self-directive principle, containing its goal inherently within its nature, and working toward this goal out of its own self-integrative need. To analyze the personality misses the significance and weakens the strength of this unitive, integrative principle. It therefore misconceives the nature of

[10] Quoted by Millin, *op. cit.*, Vol. I, p. 48.

the self-unfolding processes at work in the emergence of the individual, for it approaches these processes analytically from the outside inward, rather than as dynamic unfoldment from the inside out.

This was Smuts's holistic principle applied to its proper and primary field, the study of personality. With it, he anticipated conceptions that came to the fore in depth psychology only at a late point in its development. He anticipated the theory of wholeness presented by Alfred Adler; and Adler gladly acknowledges their community of understanding. He anticipated, in principle, the conception of the Self and the process of individuation set forth by C. G. Jung; and also, in the same way, the conception of the "integrative will" as the unifying "third principle" of personality arrived at by Otto Rank toward the end of his life.

These formulations were not present in the beginnings of psychoanalysis, but were reached as an outcome of the study of the depths of the psyche by the main authors who came after Freud. It is thus correct to say that, with his insight into the holistic nature of man, Smuts anticipated the *conclusions* that depth psychology would reach thirty years after Freud's original hypothesis; and these conclusions provide the foundational concepts that are the starting point for depth psychology in the new phase of its development, which we shall describe in later pages.

The ultimate goal of Smuts's studies, as we have seen, was to develop a scientific understanding of the creative, emergent nature of human personality. Toward this purpose, he felt it was particularly important to investigate the personality development of those who had achieved the highest realization of individuality and spiritual competence in their lives. From this, it would be possible to discover empirically and formulate scientifically the underlying principles of personality growth. We would then possess a "science of personality" capable of fulfilling the larger potentialities and aspirations of mankind. Such a "science of personality," Smuts wrote in his *Holism and Evolution,* would be "the synthetic science of human nature;" that is to say, it would not dissect man and diagnose him analytically, but it would concentrate on drawing forth the capacities of his wholeness. It would be, he said, "the crown of all the sciences." [11]

Smuts, we see, was interested in science not merely for the sake of science itself. He wanted to make use of the critical and constructive attitude of science in order to achieve an understanding that would meet the fullness of *modern man's* need. The older forms of psychology were too circumscribed to be of help in this; and so Smuts envisioned a new kind of psychology that would address itself to the goal of creatively developing the human personality. He was in this sense a precursor of the new holistic depth psychology that is now taking shape in the second half of the twentieth century.

With this purpose, Smuts worked out his conception of the holistic nature of personality in the perspective of natural evolution. In the nature of things, he was not in a position to provide a full interpretation of the human personality in depth. He did not have at his disposal at that

[11] *Holism and Evolution,* p. 285.

time the tools of understanding that were the cumulative result of research and practice in depth psychology over the period of sixty years that followed his study of Walt Whitman.[12] He himself was never able to fulfil the goal he had set, the goal of defining the specific principles of personality growth and of describing definite procedures that other individuals could follow in their quest of personal development. What he did do, however, was to mark off the *direction* in which the study of man ought to be carried; and he set criteria of fulfillment for a true *depth* psychology that would do its work in the spirit of science guided by an awareness of the wholeness and the magnitude of human personality.

Smuts did not use the term *depth psychology,* for it was not in general currency, neither in England nor in South Africa, at the time that he was writing. In fact, even the term *psychology* presented a problem for him. On the one hand it stood for the abstract intellectualism exemplified by James Ward; and on the other hand, in its psychoanalytic phase—which was much more meaningful to Smuts—it had a medical emphasis and showed a marked preconcern with the pathology of personality.

There did not seem to be a place in psychology as Smuts knew of it in the 1920's for studies that would have as their goal the creative development of personality. He therefore offered tentatively another name, "Personology," to refer to a new field of study directed toward this special

---

[12] For an integrative summary of the concepts that were the outcome of the flux in thought that followed Freud, see Progoff's *The Death and Rebirth of Psychology.*

goal. But the making of this new term was not necessary at all, for Smuts's conception of man did in fact belong inherently within the framework of psychology. This was demonstrated quite clearly after *Holism and Evolution* was published by the interest and even enthusiasm it elicited from a variety of psychologists, mainly of the Gestaltist and Hormic points of view.

The most significant support for Smuts's holistic hypothesis as an approach to the study of man came from Alfred Adler. Adler had, at that point in his work in the late 1920's, come to the conclusion that the true goal of psychology is the development of the potentialities of human nature. He was convinced, in fact, that psychology would have to reorient itself in terms of this goal even if only to fulfill its medical function of resolving the confusions of modern neurotics. And Adler saw in Smuts's holistic view of man, with its corollary of a special science devoted to personality growth, the crystallization of his own view of what psychology needs to achieve.

For many reasons, by virtue of his eminence in political and diplomatic affairs, and because of his sensitivity to the human problems of our time, Jan Christian Smuts lived as a prototype of modern man in his spiritual need and his intellectual searching. The knowledge of natural science had left a permanent mark upon him. Nothing that failed to meet its standards could remain in his personal view of the world, and he thus had had to reject the main core of traditional religious dogmas, at least as literally understood. But, at the same time, Smuts was a person who intimately knew the reality of the inner life, and knew it by glimpses and intuitions from the earliest years of his intellectual maturity. Both were true in his eyes: the hard objectivity of science and the pliant, elusive way of spiritual understanding. Somehow, he felt—and this is the thought that was with him in the years that preceded his study of Walt Whitman—these two apparent opposites will eventually be found to be only different sides of a single principle. This was the *holistic principle* which, as he remarked in his later years, remained with him all his life not only as an intellectual, interpretative theory, but as an active guiding principle both in his inner and his outer life.

The central conflict in modern thinking concerns this difficult paradoxical area where religious feeling and natural science meet and contend. Modern man often reacts to the conflict as though it were a permanent and insoluble dilemma. He represses either one side or the other. Either he represses his natural, biological side, or, as in the case of the dream of the luminous child, he represses his religious sensibilities.

With his *holistic principle* Smuts showed that science and the spirit are not irreconcilable, that an integrative, unifying way is indeed possible. Now the task remains of drawing forth this new unifying point of view, and of making it explicit in livable detail.

It is a task to be done on two levels: first conceptually, to provide a perspective and a set of hypotheses for our thinking; and secondly, in practice, to chart the variety of methods with which to meet the day-to-day problems of personality growth.

Smuts made a suggestive start in this direction, but he

left much to be explored and much still to be understood before his ultimate goal would be in sight, his goal of developing the human individual as the crowning achievement of evolution. Since he wrote his general statement of holism, many researchers have followed a path similar to his in their own fields of endeavor, fields that vary from biology to the study of civilization.[13] But where his central and encompassing goal, the study and growth of man, is concerned, it seems that the fulfillment of what Smuts envisioned lies in the realm of the new holistic depth psychology.

[13] For a striking appreciation of the impact of Smuts's work, see Arnold Toynbee's *A Study of History,* Vol. III, New York, Oxford University Press.

5 * Biology and depth psychology: the perspective of Edmund Sinnott

THE BIOLOGIST AS A MODERN MAN

The questions of what the human personality is, what the mind and the soul may be, have tantalized the curiosity of man since the earliest days of civilization. Psychology—as the science of the *psyche,* which means in its original Greek either mind or soul—represents man's disciplined attempt in the advanced stages of his culture to work out a full and integrated conception of what the intangible, non-physical realities of man's nature may be. If one judged by the mechanistic and behavioristic schools of psychology that have sought to build a "psychology without a psyche," one might not imagine this to be the case. But it is, nevertheless, true that in its origins and essence, psychology since ancient times has comprised man's civilized and sophisticated efforts to understand those aspects of his being variously referred to as his *soul,* his *mind,* his *personality.*[1]

In every period of history since the most ancient times, man has devised some kind of conception with which to explain his experiences in this elusive side of his life. Visions come to him, messages in words and images, dreams, inspirations, guidance, and warnings. Thus there have been theories of the soul as an entity separate from the body, leaving the body at night and returning so the sleeper can awaken. There have been theories of the personality as a distinct entity living through many lifetimes in many bodies, both in animal and in human forms. Animistic theories of many kinds, conceiving of the reincarnation and transmigration of personal *entities* under various forms and guises, have played a large and important role in man's attempt to understand the elusive phenomena of his inner experiences.

Often, to the modern Western mind, these conceptions seem primitive and far-fetched; that is because their starting point is so far from the naturalistic view of man that has dominated our thinking since the Darwinian theory of evolution gained acceptance. What we should bear in mind is that these vivid animistic conceptions, despite their apparent naïveté, are referring to experiences of the human psyche that reappear throughout mankind. And where the interpretation that is given may seem to us

[1] See George Sidney Brett, *History of Psychology,* one-volume ed., New York, Macmillan, 1953.

to be rather freely and even exotically imaginative, we should remember that the persons describing them are being as frank and as realistic as they are capable of being by the light of their cultural understanding. To them, who see the universe within a particular frame of reference, as Hindus and Buddhists do, to interpret certain classes of experiences of the psyche in terms of transmigration, and reincarnation is only common sense. To them it is self-evident fact, and any empiric attempt by modern man to understand the nature of the psyche must take such facts seriously into account.

Another reason why the reincarnation type of theory is difficult for the modern psychologist to comprehend is that its basis is an Oriental view of the cosmos that is strange to the Western mind. This difference reaches far into the past, and into the deepest preconceptions of Western thinking. In the Old Testament it is written in the Book of Genesis that the Ruach Elohim, the Spirit (or Breath) of God hovered over the universe; and when the human being was created, God breathed His Spirit into man. In this conception of man, then, the human spirit is inherently connected with God's own nature.

This is the view that underlies man's thinking about himself in the entire biblical tradition with all its derivatives, Jewish, Christian, and Islamic. The Breath of God has been breathed into man. God made him in His own image, and therefore there is a measure of divinity inherent in each human being.

In this biblical view, which underlies the Western conception of man, the human being is not a lonely wanderer through time and cosmos as he appears to be in the Oriental view of reincarnation. In contrast to the Oriental view of endless and impersonal rebirths, the Western individual is conceived in direct personal relation to God.

Thus the Nameless but Personal God can speak through a prophet, be he Moses, Isaiah, or Mohammed; for the prophet, as a human being, has some of the divinity of the Spirit of God already in him, waiting to be reawakened when the central experience of God comes to him. Further, in the Christian teaching, the Word, which is the Logos, is the Spirit, or Breath, of God; and here the seed of divinity in man is raised to its epitome as the Breath of God becomes incarnate in a human being. The conception of Messiahship, which is at the core of the Christian experience, harks back to the basic biblical view that the spirit of man partakes of divinity because at the moment of creation God breathed some of His Spirit into man.

Symbolic conceptions such as these are much more important and far-reaching in their effects than theological doctrines. They reach deeply into the tissue of a civilization, into the substrata of its thinking about the nature of man and his life. That is why one of the most deeply ingrained articles of Western belief has been the feeling that the human spirit partakes of divinity and is immortal. The soul is derived from God, according to the primordial biblical text and teaching. And when we set this side by side with the naturalistic view that man has emerged from the animal kingdom—the Breath of God not having hovered anywhere near the scene—we have some measure of the impact that Darwin's theory of evolution has had upon the foundations of Western thought.

It reversed Western thinking about what man's sources and resources are. Man's home is not in heaven but upon earth. His realm is the animal kingdom. And since one of the main tasks undertaken by modern biologists has been to reach the implications of the evolutionary hypothesis in every nook and cranny of nature, biology as a science has become the symbol to modern man of the new earth-centered view of life.

With this there has come the common assumption that the science of biology, like the theory of evolution, would follow a materialistic point of view. It seemed so obvious as to be taken for granted, and a cursory look at the tone of biological research in the universities would seem to confirm that view. But it leaves one very important fact out of consideration. This fact is the biologist himself.

Though his interest may be in the life of ameba, the biologist himself is a human being; and he has human concerns. His psychological roots reach back through Western civilization to the spiritual perception of man that is the heritage of the biblical tradition. If the biologist busies himself with a conception of man that negates the older view of things, it is because the new conception seems to provide more adequate answers to his questions. That was how it was when the evolutionary hypothesis first gained acceptance. It brought the best available answers to the questions then being asked about how the various species originated, how some were eliminated, and how some survived.

Important though they were, these were not the only questions that needed to be asked. Increasingly, other subjects forced themselves to the fore. Attention was turned especially to the question of the relationship between the mind and the body, and the possibility that there is some spiritually meaningful quality in human life not unrelated to the fact of natural evolution.

The various conceptions of the emergence of the *mind* in the human species could be studied by biologists in a purely professional, dispassionate way. But they had more than a professional interest in the matter. Here was involved not an abstract issue of science, but a personal need to know the nature and the meaning of human individuality. And this personal need was born of the fact that the biologist has been formed as a human being in the mold of Western civilization.

Whatever his scientific intellect may say, the modern researcher carries within himself the heritage of his cultural past, of generations that have lived in the belief that the human being possesses a dignity and a value that are unique in all creation. Philosophies of this kind are necessarily at work behind the scenes of the scientist's thinking. In the background of his mind there remains the notion that man, body and all, is somehow a spiritual being, that his life has a meaning, and that his destiny is connected in some special way with the divinity referred to in the Bible as God.

The question that came to the foreground in the wake of Darwin's discovery of evolution thus involved the reassertion of old spiritual beliefs that are now calling out and demanding recognition. Because the modern biologist is not only a biologist but also a human being, he experiences this vividly and urgently, in varying degrees according to his individual character. He is impelled then by his personal need to work out the relationship between the fact that on the one hand he feels a spiritual quality to be present in man, and on the other hand he understands biologically man's place in the order of nature.

In this search he is encouraged by an unverified but persistent suspicion that man's spiritual nature is not in conflict with his evolutionary origin, but is in fact the result of it. The two questions thus belong together. Indeed, they require each other. And it is with this awareness that a biologist of the stature of Edmond Sinnott calls for "a biology which in breadth and depth covers the *whole* of life," adding, "we must understand *life* to understand man." [2]

FROM PROTOPLASM TO PERSONALITY

Sinnott has made some particularly suggestive contributions toward understanding the unity that underlies the spiritual and biological nature of man. It is a subject that has been a lifelong concern of his. He has been en-

[2] *Mind, Matter and Man,* p. 23.

gaged in it existentially as a *modern man,* in our special sense of the term. That is to say, as a *modern man* he has been sensitive to the conflicts and confusions that have distinguished the period of history in which he lives. He has felt the issues of his time intimately within himself, and so he has been impelled to come to terms with them personally, using the equipment of his special scientific training as his tool. In doing this, he has worked toward answers that meet not only his own need but the need of his modern fellow men as well.

Sinnott has worked in this area consistently for many years, parallel to his more specialized studies in botany, a field in which he holds a position of high eminence. In the McNair Lectures delivered at the University of North Carolina, which were published under the title, *Cell and Psyche,* he opened some important doors without reaching the full implications of his growing point of view.[3] Later, in 1953, he carried his line of thought further in *Two Roads to Truth.*[4] But in two more recent books, *The Biology of the Spirit,*[5] and especially in *Matter, Mind and Man,*[6] he has crystallized his thinking in an illuminating and highly usable form.

In these later writings, Sinnott has succeeded to a significant degree in formulating an integrative concep-

[3] Edmund W. Sinnott, *Cell and Psyche,* Chapel Hill, University of North Carolina Press, 1950.

[4] *Two Roads to Truth,* New York, Viking, 1953.

[5] *The Biology of the Spirit,* New York, Viking Press, 1955, and reprinted in paperback by Compass Books in 1957.

[6] *Matter, Mind and Man,* New York, Harper & Bros., 1957, Vol. XI in the *World Perspectives* series, edited by Ruth Nanda Anshen.

tion of body and mind. He had done this not in a technical, biological form, but more generally and schematically in a way that gives orientation to our thinking. In doing so he has become the spokesman for a number of other researchers in the biological field, whose studies have been leading them in a similar direction. It is this direction of thinking that is important for us here. Without technical jargon, it opens for us a large evolutionary perspective in which to place our investigation of the creative qualities of human personality. And it provides a biological foundation for the new holistic depth psychology.

Sinnott sets the starting point of his thinking at a level even more fundamental than evolution. He reaches back to the primary material of the life process itself. He begins with *protoplasm,* the "proteinaceous, semi-liquid, flowing, formless stuff . . . which is the physical basis of life." [7]

Increasingly, the search of biologists for the ultimate substance of the life process has led in the direction of protoplasm. "It is deceptively simple in appearance," and yet, "out of it emerge the vast and varied phenomena of living organisms." [8] Not only some but *"all* problems of life come to focus" here in the basic stuff of protoplasm.

Although very significant advances in understanding it have recently been made, the question of exactly what protoplasm is still eludes biological study. A precise knowledge of its "complex physical structure and chemical composition" is much to be desired, but it is not an abso-

[7] *Matter, Mind and Man,* pp. 67, 68.
[8] *Ibid.,* p. 68.

lute necessity for understanding the general and underlying role of protoplasm in shaping the nature of man.

Sinnott makes a sharp and significant observation that
points the way in this. "Protoplasm," he says, "is not a
substance but a *system*."[9] What is important about it is not
what it *is* but what it *does*. The way in which protoplasm
functions in the life process is the most characteristic
and essential thing about it. And while we may not yet
have definite knowledge about either its physical or
chemical qualities, the manner of its operation is something we do know about. It is this aspect of protoplasm
that Sinnott interprets in developing a perspective for the
holistic study of man.

"We must regard protoplasm," Sinnott writes, "as
possessing a *pattern which so regulates the course of the
changes that go on within it that a specific form or activity
tends to result.*" [10]

The "specific form" in which protoplasm tends to
reproduce itself is of the greatest significance. Sinnott
likes to remind us that Darwin regarded morphology, the
study of forms in nature, as the very essence of biology.[11]
But in what does form consist? It is a direction of growth;
and it is a pattern of growth. But perhaps the most significant fact about it is that it varies from one organism to another.

Protoplasm is the underlying stuff fundamental to the
life process as a whole, but something within its nature

9 *Ibid.,* p. 68.
10 *Ibid.,* p. 68 (Sinnott's italics).
11 *Ibid.,* pp. 32-33.

leads it to vary its forms in individual organisms. Proto-plasm itself is amorphous, but it takes form by means of a virtual infinity of patterns of growth in nature. And once the pattern is set in, the form varies consistently.

There is, inherent in each form, an *organic pattern,* and "this organic pattern has a hereditary base." "Its roots are in a protoplasm which is specifically different in the various kinds of animals and plants. It is built up by the interaction of thousands of separate genes, each of which, as modern genetic research has shown, controls or affects some process." [12]

The genes are carriers of a particular kind of potential-ity, in each case a special pattern by which protoplasm will grow in a unique and individual form. All that they transmit is a seed, a possibility; but what is implicit in this seed is a large and continuing process of growth. Some-thing comes forth functionally from the gene that was not explicitly contained in it either physically or chemically. Something comes forth gradually, and the striking thing about it is that the pattern by which this unfoldment takes place is, in principle, always the same. Something in the genes, which transmits the forms of protoplasm, maintains a consistency of pattern according to its nature. The pattern or growth is organized and directed from within. "There is inherent in the living system," Sinnott writes, "A self-regulating quality that keeps it directed toward a definite norm or course, and the growth and activity of the organism takes place in conformity to it." [13] This internally

12 *Ibid.,* pp. 41-42.
13 *The Biology of the Spirit,* p. 64.

guided, self-consistent principle of orderedness and direction is a basic quality of protoplasm, whatever the physical basis of protoplasm may finally be determined to be.

The question then arises of how we can understand the guiding principle, the "inner protoplasmic directiveness" that is "inherent in every organism." [14] Sinnott uses, as his illustration for this, examples drawn from his special field of botany. One cannot but be impressed by the tendency of plants and trees to regenerate themselves and replace spontaneously parts that have been shorn off. "Somehow," Sinnott writes, "there must be present in the plant's living stuff, immanent in all its parts, something that represents the natural configuration of the whole, as a norm to which its growth conforms, a 'goal' toward which development is invariably directed. This insistent fact confronts us everywhere in biology."[15]

IMAGE-MAKING AND THE LIFE PROCESS

Here is a picture of the processes by which individual organisms develop. The raw stuff of life is formless protoplasm, but when it takes form it does so as a unity in which the eventual outcome of the entire process of growth is present, in principle, in the seed that is the carrier of the organism. It is as though a goal were built into the genes.

[14] *Matter, Mind and Man,* pp. 137-138.
[15] *Biology of the Spirit,* pp. 26-27.

We see instances of this "self-regulation" leading toward goals everywhere in nature. Sinnott describes a session of biological bird-watching during which he observed a hummingbird build its nest. Bit by bit, it brought its materials together, fitted them into place, and cemented them with its saliva. The bird acted like "a human craftsman, sizing up a particular problem, trying this means and that, and finally reaching a satisfactory solution. And yet this tiny bird had probably never seen a nest built, had nothing to imitate, had never learned the mechanics of nest building. This was perhaps the first nest she had ever made, and it was no different from those she might make in the years to come." [16]

Processes of this kind have generally been referred to in the past as "instinctual." But such a term covers too much and says too little that is specific. It is worth looking at much more closely.

Here, at this rudimentary level, we have the simplest instances of mental processes. These, Sinnott points out, are "the dim beginnings of mind." The instinctual building activities of the hummingbird constitute behavior moving toward a goal. They have a mental quality. They express a purposiveness that is implicit in the structure of the organism. They function *as though* they were conscious; but they were not consciously directed at all. And yet they were very truly directed in a way that is the most meaningful of all. They were directed by the self-regulating protoplasmic principle that draws each organism

16 *Matter, Mind and Man,* p. 44.

toward the goal that fulfills the process of growth inherent in its form.

We have here, Sinnott says, "the simplest sort of psychical process." It does indeed demonstrate definite "physical traits." And what is of overwhelming significance is the fact that this psych-like[17] activity derives from basic protoplasmic patterns of growth. Man's mental activity, in essence and origin, is thus "coextensive with life itself."[18]

From this, Sinnott draws the basis for his encompassing perspective, which he presents in terms of a general schematic conception of stages. "In behavior," he writes, "protoplasmic purpose grows to instinct, and with dawning consciousness this leads to thought and the higher elements of mind." [19]

The statement that psychologic processes are "coextensive with life itself" has the very largest implications. We are accustomed to thinking of mind and body as though they are in some sense separate entities, either influencing one another or proceeding side by side. In the mechanistic view, the processes of the body determine the development of the mind. In the vitalist view, mind is the creative factor and has the power to alter physical processes. A compromise view is interactionism, which holds that body and mind influence each other. And *psycho-physical parallelism* con-

[17] C. G. Jung, following Driesch, uses the term *psychoid,* which by its Greek derivation means psych-like. See Progoff, *The Death and Rebirth of Psychology,* pp. 167-168.
[18] *Matter, Mind and Man,* p. 43.
[19] *Ibid.,* pp. 43-44.

ceives of mind and body as the two distinct sides of a single coin.

The organismic view of man that Sinnott sets forth makes it possible to see beyond these dichotomies. His underlying conception is that protoplasm, the basic life stuff, is essentially a system moving toward goals, goals that are built into the protoplasmic stuff of each living organism according to its nature.[20]

In the course of moving toward its goals, the protoplasmic system develops mind and consciousness as essential aspects of its life growth. These are inherent in the process of moving toward goals. Mind and body are both expressions of protoplasm moving toward a purpose in terms of the nature of a particular organism. "The body results," Sinnott says, "from the developmental activities of protoplasm which incorporates matter into a self-regulating living system, and mind acts on this same matter by regulating its behavior. The *psycho-physical parallelism,* so long and earnestly debated, in this sense, is not a parallelism but an identity." And Sinnott adds, "This idea is not new but to the orthodoxies of our day it is still a startling one."[21]

Perhaps this idea is not so much startling as overwhelming, especially when one considers its implications and the blocked fields of study that it opens anew. The entire question of the mind-body relationship may now be approached with fresh understanding in the realization

[20] *Ibid.,* p. 205.
[21] *Ibid.,* p. 76.

that mind and body have their source together in the basic protoplasmic life process. Both are "coextensive with life itself;" and with this conception the study of healing, of extrasensory perception, and the variety of unexplained phenomena that have been lumped into the field of "parapsychology" may become understandable in a new light. It is a conception of man that is bound to have repercussions in many fields of study, but the most fundamental of these concerns the nature of consciousness and the depth levels of personality.

"Let us then," Sinnott writes, "for purposes of this discussion, define mind as *whatever directs the development and activity of an organism toward goals set up within its living stuff.*" [22]

Of course this is not a conventional definition of "mind." It does not correspond by any means to the usage either of philosophers or psychologists. But Sinnott's interpretation of the term in this connection has a particular aptness. In all the life process, in the simplest plants and animals, there is a movement toward a goal. If obstacles appear, something in the essence of protoplasm works to overcome the difficulties, to circumvent them or adapt to them, in order to reach the ultimate goal that is built into the protoplasmic nature of the organism. The organism spontaneously regulates its own behavior *as though it knew* what its goal was, and *as though it knew* what it actually had to do in order to achieve its goal.

There is no consciousness here in the sense of human awareness. The hummingbird is not conscious of the fact

[22] *Ibid.,* p. 85, Sinnott's italics.

that it is building a nest; it does not consciously choose to use this kind of twig instead of that one to build its nest this size and no larger. It makes no conscious choices, but it builds its nest to specifications that always meet the requirements of its goals. It acts, in other words, *as though* it were conscious, as though a mind were at work. And so Sinnott defines "mind" not in terms of human consciousness as is usually done, but in terms of the inner regulation and directiveness toward goals that work within protoplasm in all the species of nature. This tendency to work toward goals is the basis of "mind" as it appears in man in advanced stages of development where we speak of it as "consciousness."

How does "mind" express itself at the high levels of human mental growth? In man, the basic protoplasmic process of working toward goals that are built into the organism has become conscious of its own activity. Man is a self-conscious being. The individual works to achieve purposes that derive ultimately from the same instinctual levels as the bird building a nest: but he has conscious techniques at his disposal and he works with an awareness of the process as a whole. He is, to this degree, not spontaneously fulfilling the protoplasmic goals of life— goals that are real before thought is taken—but he is working toward goals that he "thinks" he wants. Consciously, he seeks goals that do not come out of his basic protoplasmic nature, but which are the derivative goals of his consciousness. It was in reference to this point in the development of man's consciousness that both of the depth psychologists, C. G. Jung and Otto Rank, issued their basic warnings to *modern man* that he beware of getting out of touch with his basic nature through the hyperdevelopment of self-consciousness.

The purposive and formative tendency inherent in proto-plasm, which is the seed of psychic processes in man, appears in two different aspects in the human species. One is self-conscious awareness. The other is the spontaneous expression of the goals that are latent in the living stuff of personality. "The protoplasmic pattern immanent in the egg or in any cell, to which the various stages in development and finally the structure of the mature individual will conform, is the prototype of a purpose, and finally of an idea, that is immanent in the cells of the brain." [23]

In saying this, Sinnott indicates the stages by which the purposes that are eventually pursued by man consciously emerge from their latent position in the very structure of the egg. Ultimately, on the level of consciousness, they are expressed as an *idea,* but the basis of the idea is ever the nonconscious unfolding of the "protoplasmic pattern."

These "ideas," which are the crystallization of the primary purposes working in the "egg," might better be described as *images.* The bird building its nest has no *idea* of what it is doing, but it can truly be said that an image belonging not to the mind as such, but to the organism as a whole, is drawing the process of nest-building forward. The process of making images, which is what the term *imagination* really involves, means much more than fantasy.

[23] *Ibid.,* p. 91.

It is an integral part of, indeed is an essential instrument of the basic protoplasmic process in man.

In this fundamental and dynamic sense as the image-making that is the necessary psychologic side of the basic process of protoplasmic unfoldment, imagination does indeed have "its roots in life." It expresses, as Sinnott says, "a *spontaneous* quality . . . in man's living stuff." [24] And this spontaneity is nothing less than the form that protoplasm is taking in the individual organism. The form contains the eventual purpose, the direction of growth, planted in the primary seed of the life process. It is represented as a basic image that is present in the egg as a picture of its potentiality. What the egg can become, what a human being can become, depends upon the fulfillment of this image, its ability to grow and to become real. At each step along the road, a new image comes forth to express that particular stage in the individual's growth. It is a continuous process of image-making that takes place in a variety of aspects and degrees, varying from creative imagination to fantasy and dreams. All of this has the greatest psychologic significance. This process of image-making, which takes place on the deepest levels of the unconscious, is actually the psychologic side of the life process by which the human organism grows toward the form and goal of his individuality.

In the framework of thinking that Sinnott has developed, we have seen that the ultimate goal toward which protoplasm moves is personality. The formation and integration of personality is thus the goal toward

24 *Ibid.*, p. 123.

which image-making, the depth process of imagination, is heading. This is so because of the nature of protoplasm in the human species. The basis for this understanding is an essentially biologic insight, but it supports and amplifies some of the most important hypotheses with which depth psychology works.

We shall come to these points a little later in our study, but we may remark here that what is involved is not merely the analysis of the content of image-making—i.e., the meaning of symbols, and so on—but the nature of the process of image-making and its relation to the growth of personality. This leads to the question of the best procedures for working with images; and this opens one of the crucial areas where depth psychology can make a major contribution to the development of modern man. This is a subject to which we shall soon return in greater detail, for the juncture where Sinnott's biological perspective meets the depth study of the psyche is a point of fruitful union in the development of modern man.

At this point in our inquiry, we wish merely to recall the development of thought that we have been following so far in tracing the peregrination of modern man. In Jan Christian Smuts we saw an individual straining to draw together the scientific evidence for natural evolution, and his intimate perception of the creativity of the human spirit. His answer took the form of the principle of holism, the theory that evolution is a procession of ever more advanced *wholes,* whose ultimate achievement lies in the full development of human personality.

In Edmund Sinnott a similar problem and a similar desire came together. Here, however, one important ingredient was added: the disciplined knowledge of a specialist in biological science. Here again a conception of *wholeness* shows itself to be fundamental. Each organism is a unity carrying forward the life process in accordance with its nature. Life is protoplasm, and protoplasm moves toward goals that are unknown in origin; but they are profound in their vistas, creative in their achievements, and great in their destiny.

The ultimate destiny of protoplasm is human personality. Here, as in life itself, much is dark. But here too, as in the primal patterns of protoplasmic growth, something works in the darkness, casting forth images that become visible and meaningful in the light of experience. Out of the darkness of life and in the midst of the depths of still unformed personality, the human spirit emerges.

This is the core of the understanding we derive from the work of Edmund Sinnott. Man is a creature born in the world of nature and functioning in accordance with its laws. Precisely because this is so, Sinnott tells us, the human being reaches beyond himself toward spiritual vistas. The unboundedness of his personality is the highest achievement of evolution. Our task now is to see what is involved and implied in this entire process, to see what meanings and goals it brings to the life of modern man, and to find the methods and techniques by which its possibilities can be productively fulfilled in our time. These are the purposes of the discussions that follow.

6 * *The urge toward ongoing life*

MAN BETWEEN EARTH AND HEAVEN

What are the natural principles by which personality emerges in man? What is the meaning of the creative process that is at work here? While man is a creature of the animal kingdom, does the spiritual quality of personality have implications that point beyond the sphere of nature with which we are directly in contact? Is there a transpersonal reality that is reflected in man and that becomes perceivable at the higher stages of personality development? And are there any practices, techniques, and methods of procedure by which the individual in modern times can work toward this goal, and by which he can assist the growth of those capacities of individuality that fulfill the evolutionary process?

As human beings living in the modern age, we cannot take as the starting point of our thinking any view of man other than as a being who is part of nature. But the naturalistic and Darwinian conception is only the foundation upon which we build our awareness and understanding. The evolutionary view of man provides the base of operations where our inquiry takes its origin and has its fixed point of reference; but it should not be permitted to become a fence that sets boundaries round our thinking. It is vitally important that, while we study man as an earthbound being, we keep our vistas open in all directions and be sensitive to all the varied aspects of human life.

It is interesting to note the fact that the most profound books of spiritual teaching take as their starting point the earthly nature of man. This is their basis, and the model from which they draw their larger inferences. So, for example, the anonymous author of *The Cloud of Unknowing* pointed out that man "is not made bending toward the earth as all other animals are, but is made upright in the direction of heaven." "And why is this so?" he asks. "In order to represent in physical form the spiritual work of the soul, a work that is possible only for those who are upright spiritually and are not spiritually bent toward the ground." [1]

There is particular meaning in the fact that man is an

1 *The Cloud of Unknowing,* translated with an introductory commentary by Ira Progoff, New York, Julian Press, 1957, LXI:4, p. 208.

erect creature. With his feet, it is said, he holds down the earth; and with his head and shoulders, he sustains the heavens. Thus man, rooted in earth, by his very nature reaches upward and beyond his primary earthliness. "If a man has himself firmly in hand and stands solidly upon the earth," a Hasidic proverb says, "then his head reaches up to heaven." [2]

In this sense man is the connecting link of the universe. In him heaven and earth come together. It is a union that is possible only because both the earthly and the spiritual are present in the nature of man. He comes from the earth, but he stands upright. And this symbolic aspect of his physical structure, his posture with respect to the cosmos, reveals the elusive twofold quality of human existence that must always be remembered in the study of man.

With these reflections in mind, let us now turn our attention to the large, encompassing process by which the human individual develops toward the goal of integral personality that is inherent in his nature. Thinking in evolutionary terms, we wish to follow the genetic process of growth that moves in this direction; and for this we have a choice of two possible procedures. One is to trace the intimate life of the person from his moment of birth as a hapless infant in the strange environment of his family. The other possibility is to study the human being as a member of a species in the animal kingdom, and to follow the growth of individuality within that context. These two starting points differ rather widely in the

[2] *Ten Rungs, Hasidic Sayings,* collected and edited by Martin Buber, New York, Schocken Books, 1947, p. 40.

perspective they bring to the study of man. One is the direct, frontal approach to individuality, beginning with the birth of the child, the point at which the physical emergence of individuality becomes tangible and clear, the point also where social contact visibly begins.

By contrast, the other approach to man through the study of the human species takes an indirect road. Its goal also is an understanding of personality, but it reaches back to a point before individuality has made its appearance. It wants to find first the underlying traits that are common to the species as a whole; then to study the specific forms in which they develop in the varieties of individuality. It involves a reaching back to the impersonal and the nonindividual in man, in order to gain access to the fundamental sources and components of the individual personality.

It turns out, too, that though these starting points seem to be opposites, they actually fit together very closely. They complement each other, and without both of them the study of man is incomplete. It is important to keep this in mind because the modern urge to be only empirical in the study of man often results in an overemphasis on what is tangible and visible. The modern mind is so anxious to show that it is dealing with things that are clearly perceivable rather than with what is obscure that it inadvertently limits itself to the surface of things, and traps itself in superficiality. And yet, paradoxically, in the study of man it is just what is obscure, intangible, and difficult to lay hands on that is most important to understand. It is necessary that we reach the nonpersonal

—and eventually the transpersonal—sources of personality if we are to comprehend the growth of the specific individual, the child visibly moving toward maturity.

THE ORGANS OF SURVIVAL IN MAN

The crowning outcome of evolution, we have seen, is the individual, the emergence of the integral person. But the raw materials of personality are the very opposite of individuality. They are, in a sense, preindividual, for they include the structure and capacities of the organism as these are present in the species as a whole. The basic processes of personality are no more personal than the circulation of the blood or the knitting of the bones, for they are characteristics of all humans as members of their species.

When we ask what these most fundamental traits of the human species are, we have to think back to that dim moment in time when man emerged from the turmoil of evolution with the essentials of his present form. Many other species were eliminated in the fierce animal struggle for survival. They could not meet the test of competition and so they became extinct. But the human species was able to make good its survival in the midst of this struggle, and the qualities with which it succeeded in preserving its existence amid the brute conditions of nature are the qualities that have remained in man's inherited constitution. Other traits and qualities have been added in the course of history, and these may be transmitted from generation to generation by means of cultural inheritance. But the basic structure and characteristics of the human organism as it starts afresh in the seed of each embryo are those with which man was able to achieve survival as a distinct species.

The basic principle at work in the protoplasm of the human species is the drive for the preservation and continuance of life. This has been spoken of as the instinct of self-preservation, but it seems to involve much more than a concern for the protection of the individual. It extends beyond the individual to the species, and beyond the species to the preservation of life itself.

A strong *survival drive* is basic to human nature, for without this there would be nothing else; and for this very reason it is much more than a human characteristic. It is inherent in all the forms of life that have taken part in the struggles of evolution. Each species has worked for its own survival instinctively, blindly, clumsily, fruitlessly, some succeeding, some disappearing from view. In each species the life principle has worked to sustain itself, and where possible to perpetuate itself. It is as though there is inherent in protoplasm, in the very substance of life itself, a drive working for the perpetuation of life.

The *survival drive* is basic for all species, but in man it expresses itself in a variety of intricately developed forms. It does this in combination with the other primary traits and capacities with which the human species emerged from the vortex of evolution.

As we have seen in our discussion of Edmund Sinnott,

the protoplasm is ever moving toward a purpose, toward a goal implicit in its structure. In the effect it has upon the life process, this directedness functions as though it were a *guiding image* present and working in the organism. It is as though the seed contains an image of what it will become if it is able to reach the maturity of its species. This is the unfolding meaning of each organism inherent in the organism itself.

In simpler species we say it is *as though* a mind were at work as the organizing factor. Indeed, a mind *is* there; but still only in principle. In the human species the *guiding images* that are active in the seed of protoplasm have advanced to the point where they are able to communicate themselves. They become perceivable by the organism itself, and they are expressed with varying degrees of clarity and emotion. They may take visual form as in dreams; or they may take intellectual forms, as in ideas and conscious goals. They may be in contact with the reality of sensory experience; or they may present an unraveling of self-generated fantasies. But whatever their aspect and quality, they represent *what the psyche is* as it manifests itself. They are the specific forms in which the psyche comes forth in human development and takes its place in the forefront of evolution.

Why is a psyche necessary? The answer suggested by Alfred Adler was that without a psyche man would not have been able to survive in the struggle among the species. From the point of view of physical strength and agility, man is inferior to other species in the animal kingdom. He could survive in the competition of evolution only if some additional faculty would come forth and balance his physical weakness. This, Adler says, was the psyche. It developed in answer to the physical inferiority of man, following the principle that Adler called *compensation*. Compensation, as Adler interpreted it, is the balancing principle in all organisms and the promoter of growth in evolution. By means of it, according to his theory, the psyche developed in man beyond the minimal stage in which it appears in other species; and man was enabled not only to make good his survival but to establish his sovereignty in the animal kingdom.

Adler's theory leads a step further. Because of his physical inferiority compared to other animals, man could not survive as an individual but only by banding together with others of his species. Once again man's weakness had to be compensated for, this time by a sense of group belonging and group activity. Adler spoke of this as *social feeling*, by which he means a sense of connection to others. This social quality is now inherent in man, Adler says, because without it man could not survive as a species.

The theory of compensation is certainly not the whole story where an explanation of evolution is concerned; but there is considerable merit to the underlying point of Adler's hypothesis. We might, perhaps, formulate it more simply and say that, *if* the inner-directiveness of protoplasm had not developed in man into the active consciousness of a psyche, and *if* man had not been by nature a gregarious being, his physical inferiorities would have been fatal weaknesses in the struggles of the animal world. There are thus, inherent in the seed of the human organism, three main attributes: the *survival drive,* a *psyche,* and an inherent *sociality.* Without these, man could not have preserved his identity as a species. With them his life has unfolded in its endless permutations through history; and they remain the basic components and potentialities of his nature now in the modern age.

Of these three basic qualities with which the human species established its position in evolution, the *survival drive* is the most fundamental. The other two, man's *psyche* and his *sociality,* are essentially organs in the human being that support the underlying will to live and enable it to maintain itself.

The relationships of these three are exceedingly varied. Because their roots reach deep into human nature while their ramifications on the surface level of behavior change dynamically, the paths of their relationships are very difficult to follow. The connections and disconnections of the *psyche, sociality,* and the *survival drive* are subtle and elusive to trace. Nonetheless, they comprise the essential core of man's experience in civilization. They shape the main content of his life as a personal and as a historic being.

The difficulties of individual existence in modern times, the problems of living that have been interpreted in terms of neurosis and anxiety, arise essentially from the disconnection of these three components in human nature. The varieties of breakdown in the connectedness necessary to hold them together have been diagnosed as medical problems. But the harmonious connection and productive relationship of these three can readily be re-established, and with this the creative growth of personality becomes possible once again. It then shows itself to be a question not of diagnosing pathology but of reaffirming the holistic nature of man.

The task of bringing modern man into connection with himself, into connection with the deep sources of life within him, involves the establishment of an integral relationship among the three inherent qualities of the human organism: the survival drive, the psyche, and sociality. Rightly conceived, the task is not a difficult one, for the life process itself brings it to pass. Integral personality is built into the seed of protoplasm in the human species, and it comes into being when man is able to permit himself to be what it has always been his nature to become. His survival drive, his psyche with its multiplicity of manifestations, and his basic sociality provide the means by which integral personality may be reached. We therefore now turn to look at them more closely.

THE SURVIVAL DRIVE AND ITS EXTENSIONS

The survival drive in man expresses itself in many different aspects. In its most elemental form it is simply a *will to live*. It is not a conscious wish to live, not even an unconscious wish. It is a dark, driving urge to be part of the life process. It is in no sense an acquired desire, but a blind striving inherent in the basic life stuff of protoplasm in the organism.

In this primal aspect, the survival drive has sometimes been described as an instinct for self-preservation. The individual organism, it is said, obeys an urge simply to maintain its existence regardless of its meaning or its conditions. The life of the species is not at stake on this level; only the life of the individual organism. But it is by means of the individual organism that the species survives, and that the life process as a whole continues itself.

The individual organism is the bearer of life, not only for himself but for the life process throughout nature. In some dark way, this seems to be known by every organism. It strives to maintain its life, but it is also ready to surrender its life in the service of a larger life continuity. There are a great many examples of this in nature, of animals that perform instinctive life-enhancing acts, of mating or of child rearing, when these acts lead directly to their own demise. Yet they do these willingly. It is as though the survival drive in protoplasm identifies itself not alone with the individual organism in which it happens to find itself, but with the fullness of the life process.

Since this is so, what has been called the instinct for self-preservation must be understood in a large, extensive sense. The organism striving to defend its life and continue it is answering a protoplasmic call that refers not only to the bodily existence of the particular individual but to the maintenance of life wherever the stuff of life is found. The true instinct that we find, then, is not for *self*-preservation but for *life*-preservation.

Clear instances of this occur all through the animal kingdom; and it is especially marked in the human species where even the dimmest beginnings of civilization have appeared. The lower species, acting without consciousness, live out their protoplasmic pattern blindly destroying themselves as part of the continuity of life. But man does this knowingly and willingly under a great many circumstances, and in a wide variety of forms.

Essentially the survival drive, whether in man or in the simplest form of protoplasm, is life continuing itself. The difference between man and the simpler species is that in man the image-making faculty of his psyche, together with the strength of his social feelings, provide new contexts and new avenues of meaning, along which life may extend itself in and through the individual.

When we keep in mind that what has been called the instinct for self-preservation must be interpreted more generally to mean *life*-preservation, that it is the instinctual means by which life extends itself, we can appreciate the variety of forms that the survival drive takes. The human being first feels impelled to preserve the life he experiences immediately in his own body, but he may extend his feeling of identity beyond his immediate self. The simplest and most pervasive form of such an extension of the self in others is in having children, and in caring for them. In this, there is a semblance of an actual bodily continuation because of the "blood" tie; but the most important factor is the social feeling of connection, which is the cultural form in which the nurture of life by the parents is practiced.

In this connection, a primary derivative of the survival drive is what Thorstein Veblen aptly called the *paren-*

tal bent in man. By this phrase Veblen very perceptively intended something more inclusive than an urge to motherhood in the female and an urge to sexual release in the male. The *parental bent* is a proclivity in the human species to continue life, that is, to express the survival drive in a way that not only procreates life but nurtures and maintains it. It is more than an instinct of fatherhood and motherhood. It is a concern for the care of life that reaches beyond specific sexuality to parentage, which is an urge to succor life. It is an expression of the Survival Drive in the species that gives to the individual organism an active role in maintaining the continuity of life. And we should note that it is because the parental bent is so fundamental a drive in man that he has developed as a social being. The proclivity to nurture life through parentage requires a social situation and leads inevitably to a pattern of family organization in one cultural context or another.[3]

The *survival drive* extends itself in progressive stages. It strives for the preservation of life, first in the physical body. Then, surrendering that, it works to maintain life through a child with whom there is direct physical connection, for the child is a fruit of the body of the parent. But this too fails, for the child's body is no more durable than the parent's. It often happens that the child does not survive his parents, and in the act of burying his child (or

[3] For a description of what the term "parental bent" meant to Veblen in the full context of his social evolutionary thinking, see Thorstein Veblen, *The Instinct of Workmanship and the State of the Industrial Arts*, New York, Viking, 1957.

whatever death rite his culture prescribes), the parent is forced to find a channel for his survival drive other than "blood" survival through his children.

It often happens, too, that the parent loses control of his child to some greater authority, and this happens not only in primitive and tribal cultures but in modern times as well. The tribe may conscript a child for service in a particular ritual; it may dedicate him to the service of a particular god or goddess beyond the control of the parent; or it may press him into service for warfare in the defense of the tribe or for the glorification of its name. Then, once again, the survival drive must find another channel, one that will take into account the dim and often repressed realization that lies in the background of all of this: that eventually the child must die just as the parent must die, for all are human beings and therefore mortal. The new channel must be of a more encompassing nature, large enough to include the child within the parent's perspective of survival.

The new form of belief that carries the survival drive is essentially an extension of the "blood" connection of the parent and child. It makes the survival unit, not the parent of the child as such, but the larger family which includes them. This may be the tribe, or a group of tribes, a nation, or some conception of a "race." Then, though the body of the parent or the child may be destroyed, a larger, stronger unit endures; and the individual who died survives in this. The totem lives on. The gods who guide a people live on forever, and it is in them that the survival drive of the individual is fulfilled. If a man dies heroically in warfare, or even if he dies peacefully while carrying out the canons of conduct of the community, he can feel assured of survival anonymously in the ongoing life of his tribe.

This kind of identification of the individual with the group permits only a very dim sense of individuality. The person here is altogether encompassed by the group. Ultimately, he is fused into it so completely that the group's life is his life. He perceives no distinction, and so he can believe without doubting that his own survival is as great as and as everlasting as the survival of the group.

Such complete absorption of the individual in the life of the tribe belongs to a rather rudimentary stage of civilization, but remnants and reassertions of it have played a significant role in modern history. The tribal adventurism of fascism as Mussolini espoused it in Ethiopia is only one of the more articulate expressions of it during the period of the second World War.

It seems, however, that such systems of belief, which swallow the individual whole, are seldom able to endure for any significant historical time. The sense of individuality that is inherent in man is much too strong to permit it. The organism cannot function well enough that way. The feeling that each individual is somehow unique, integral, whole unto himself, an entity that preserves its existence despite the apparent destruction of the body, comes ever to the fore of man's life, and brings about a large variety of conceptions to meet the urgent requirements of the survival drive. The kind of tribalism that gives the individual a measure of worldly immortality, but at the cost of obliterating him, is seldom capable of maintaining itself for long, although it is still capable of some devastating flurries in the modern world. In its stead, there arise much more subtle forms of belief, varying from spiritualistic religions to the pursuit of science; but they are all directed toward the goal of fulfilling the survival drive in the individual person.

Conceptions of life that recognize the reality of the individual replace the primal fusion of the person and the tribe. Metaphysically, these conceptions cover the whole spectrum of possible beliefs. In fact, if it has seemed to us that man's ideas about life and death, primitive and modern, are remarkable for the range of their imagination, the reason is that the pressures of the survival drive have taxed the ingenuity of the psyche to the utmost.

The image-making faculty of the psyche—of which we shall speak more in detail shortly—has received its strongest and most persistent challenge from man's protoplasmic need to believe that his connection to life will not be rudely sundered, but will continue through time in a personally meaningful way. Consequently, the cosmologic beliefs of mankind present a seemingly endless permutation of images and ideas, all designed to quiet the mind of a human being when he reflects upon the death of a relative or a friend, and muses about the possibilities lurking behind his own demise. The strength of the survival drive gives a particular importance to beliefs about the nature of death. And these beliefs must meet one strict criterion above all others. Only those beliefs about death will endure that make life effective, meaningful, and livable in the here and now.

With these requirements, and within these limitations, an imposing variety of conceptions has accumulated in the course of history to provide the individual human being with a channel of expression for his protoplasmic need to feel connected to the continuity of life.

By far the largest category of these beliefs belong to the realm of religion. Fundamental here is the belief in an individual soul, as a soul substance or soul entity of some kind. To reach this stage of thinking, it is necessary first that the individual be liberated from the fusion of person and tribe of which we have spoken, and that his mind or spirit be accorded a certain autonomy or identity of its own. That is the case in all the advanced religions that stem from the Bible; and it is true also of the Hindu-Buddhist-Taoist traditions of the East.

With the observation that the physical body loses its potency and disintegrates after death, the survival drive turns first to a spiritual, or at least nonphysical, dimension to express itself. Thus we have beliefs in a life after death, a Heaven and a Hell, where rewards and punishments may be meted out. The variety of beliefs in this area is very great, ranging from the ancient Greek and Egyptian to the Hebrew-Christian view, and including many preliterate beliefs in a life beyond death.

Of great importance also in many portions of the world is the belief in the transmigration of souls. As a general conception of the continuity of life and the interconnections of all forms of life in nature, this is a view that is widely held, especially in more primitive communities. Comparable to it, but usually expressed on a much more sophisticated level of thought, is the theory of reincarnation. Here, the survival drive finds a clear and strong expression, for reincarnation asserts the unending continuity of individual lives in the world.

In the world-view of reincarnation, the forms of life change, but the connection remains. The identity of personality is not severed through all the aeons of time; and in this sense, reincarnation is a perfect expression of the survival drive in man. In its view of things, the individual does truly survive. He lives on, not in an unknowable realm of spirit, or Heaven, as in other religious views, but man survives in the same world of flesh and blood in which he has already lived, returning to meet new challenges and fulfill new roles in many different times and circumstances.

Like certain forms of belief in transmigration, reincarnation also has a didactic aspect, for there is the implication that the condition of future rebirths will vary according to the merit with which one has lived in his present incarnation. There is thus a moralistic aspect here, closely related to the Hindu notion of Karma, as dealing out pleasures and pains in future existences as the consequences of conduct in the present life.

The conception of Karma bears an interesting relationship to the survival drive. In the Hindu-Buddhist view of life, the ultimate goal is to bring about a cessation of the endless rounds of rebirth that are forecast in its view of reincarnation. Karma is the metaphysical principle of necessity, and until the effects of human desire have been overcome, ever new incarnations are inevitable in accordance with the Karma of the individual. The goal, however, is to be freed from rebirth. This would mean to die in the flesh and be born no more.

This view of life might seem to be an attempt to negate the survival drive in man. Actually, it is an attempt to fulfill it on a transcendent dimension. Nirvana does not bring an end to human survival, but it is rather the establishment of a permanent condition of survival for the person who has overcome the attachment to human desires. All these attachments are viewed as a veil of illusion, and when they are overcome, truth, which is eternal, is established. Nirvana, the highest Hindu goal, is beyond time. It is a reaching for the timelessness of eternity, and thus a most subtle expression of the survival drive carried to its logical extreme in terms of a metaphysical perception of reality. Comparable examples of this pursued from other conceptual viewpoints would be the Tantric-Taoist text, *The Secret of the Golden Flower,* and the varied attempts of the alchemists to secure the "pearl of great price" in their symbolic labors.

The goal of Nirvana as a religious attempt to fulfill the protoplasmic urge in man to establish an enduring connection to life is a prototype of many other philosophic views that express the survival drive in terms of a striving for truth and timelessness. An excellent instance of this in the history of Western thought was Baruch Spinoza's effort to achieve knowledge "in the light of eternity." His was a strong dedication to life, but he sought to establish his connection to life beyond the transitoriness of things, seeking to reach the level of ultimate truth and timelessness as far as his understanding permitted.

In the same tradition, and closer to our own day in terms of language and spirit, was Albert Einstein's experience of the unity of music and mathematics. He felt both to be beyond time in a realm of truth and universal principles. And this was the dedication of his life, to participate in eternity by unraveling the mysteries of the underlying unity of life.

To dwell in the eternal is the ultimate spiritual expression of the survival drive; for there, it may be said, enduring survival is truly established. There are many forms of this: the Heaven of the Christian, the Nirvana of the Hindu, the timeless truth of Spinoza and Einstein.

When a person lives in terms of what he deeply feels to be an imperishable reality, his survival drive has found a full and satisfying expression. It may be upon the rather exalted plane of the examples we have mentioned, the religious seer, the dedicated philosopher, the scientific seeker for truth. But it may be also in the more prosaic terms of the individual who fulfills his urge for survival in the person of his children, or by participating in his country's struggle for power. It may be found also in the faith of the person who prepares for Heaven, or who awaits a new opportunity for life in his next incarnation. Or it may show itself in the person who labors to create a work of art, a painting, a piece of sculpture, or some other tangible, enduring object in which the urgings of his survival drive may find expression.

THE FORMS OF QUALITATIVE SURVIVAL

From this discussion, which is intended only as an introduction to the subject, we can see how the survival drive transforms itself in the course of finding channels through which it can express itself. The basis of the survival drive is an urge for life-preservation inherent in protoplasm. As it develops, however, enlarging its scope from the rudimentary *parental bent* of man to the varieties of political and religious identification of which we have spoken, it draws ever larger fields of understanding and belief into its sphere. The urge to experience the ongoingness of life, to feel deeply that one is an active participant in the continuity of the life process, soon reaches beyond the possibility of believing, literally, in the survival of the body after its death. The body disintegrates; that can be seen and cannot be denied. The preservation of life must therefore take place on another level. Survival is then not survival of the same physical life process that had its origins in protoplasm. It is survival on a different plane of experience, and many are the forms that it takes. Life preserves itself by transforming itself.

Once the hope of literal bodily survival is surrendered, the field opens limitlessly for realms of experience in which the survival drive can be expressed. Survival is no longer defined in terms of physical phenomena. The goal implicit in the survival drive is immortality or eternity and, set in that perspective, the body has much too brief and transitory an existence. In fact, since timelessness is the criterion, whatever physical objects may be involved in the work of achieving survival are of secondary significance. Of primary importance is the perception of the dimension of reality upon which the survival drive is felt to be fulfilled. It is not a question of physical survival, but of *qualitative survival* in terms of meaningful experiences of the forms the life process takes as it continues beyond the physical level.

In accordance with this, we find that in the history of civilization the survival drive is expressed in a very large variety of *survival forms.* The survival form in any given time and place is the framework of thinking and belief in which a human being's feeling of ongoing participation in the life process is experienced and understood. Essentially, the various survival forms are based upon large symbolic conceptions of the nature of reality. They reach down to the fundamental assumptions of the nature of life. So, for example, the Christian vision of Heaven and Hell, the Soul, and the requirements for salvation are a particular survival form; also, the world view of reincarnation is a survival form; so also is the tribalism that fulfills the survival drive of the individual in the power exploits of the nation.

When the survival form is securely believed in, events that would otherwise be unthinkable become possible.

Thus, in the Messianic religious frenzies that periodically recur in Western civilization, as they did in primitive Christianity, in medieval Jewish Frankism, and in various nineteenth-century Protestant sects, business people who had always been engaged in accumulating wealth gave their worldly goods away in the expectation of redemption and resurrection. They did so because they truly felt their personal *survival* was at stake.

Again, the Moslem *assassins* engaged in their "holy" warfare gladly sacrificed their lives in combat, for they believed that their immortality was thereby assured. And in modern times, the Marxist who is convinced that history inexorably requires the victory of the proletariat willingly sacrifices his worldly goods and pleasures to the "cause." He believes that he is thereby participating in the true and enduring reality of life. In fact, the religious intensity of Marxist activity, which seems like fanaticism to the unfriendly eyes of capitalists and democrats, is only an indication of how fully the survival drive is engaged in the survival form of Marxism; and it is a measure also of its demonic potency on the modern political scene.

Survival forms are mainly social and religious in nature, and their reality is stated in ultimate or metaphysical terms. Their function in the economy of human nature is to provide the framework of beliefs in which the feeling of enduring connection to life can be experienced in a strong and meaningful way. When survival forms, whatever their specific content, are securely placed in the thoughts and emotions of a people, they bring a quality of social conviction that gives a dynamic resiliency to the community as a whole. This is one reason why some religious and political groups are able to act with such impressive buoyancy of spirit despite outer circumstances that would be depressing and discouraging to others. At the present time, Jehovah's Witnesses are an excellent example of this. Their view of the world is expressed in a securely believed survival form, a vision of the resurrection to come, understood in the light of their rereading of prophecy; and with this connection to enduring life, the protoplasmic survival drive in them is freed for vigorous expression.

There is a great deal to be gained from the close study of survival forms in the history of civilization. We can learn much about the nature of society by observing the rhythms with which such forms are accepted, held, and eventually rejected. Of especial importance is the relation between the survival form dominant in a culture and the stability and general capacity of individual personalities who are brought within its influence. One pair of conclusions seems certain, and these conclusions provide excellent starting points from which considerable further investigation may fruitfully be done. That is, that when a survival form is well integrated into the personality and is deeply experienced, it places great funds of energy at the disposal of the individual; and when, conversely, no survival form is functioning so that the survival drive at the depths of the psyche has no channel of expression, the individual feels cut off from life, confused, devoid of meaning, and he becomes an easy victim of anxiety.

In this book, one of our main goals is to provide the

tools of thinking, the concepts, insights, and frame of reference with which these alternate possibilities can be understood. And especially our desire is to show the way by which in actual practice the survival drive in modern man may become free to establish a creative connection to life. In order to accomplish this practical goal, we shall have to look closer now at the specific contents that comprise the various survival forms.

We have already seen that the underlying motive force behind the survival forms is the survival drive whose source is deep in the protoplasmic core of the human organism. The particular beliefs that carry this basic urge forward can be stated as definite ideas capable of being consciously defined and lucidly articulated. But their ultimate origin and basis are deeply unconscious. They are derived from the symbolism produced by the ingenious fertility of the image-making faculty of the deep psyche. In quest of new light upon this dark and important subject, we have called upon the joint resources of organismic biology and the new, holistic depth psychology. With these we now turn the focus of our attention on the principles and processes involved in the growth of what we here call the *Organic Psyche*.

7 * *The organic psyche and its contents*

THE SEED OF WHOLENESS

What do we mean when we speak of the *organic psyche?* It is by no means a special area or a separate entity marked off from the rest of the human being; and yet it does operate in terms of principles that are distinctly its own. The organic psyche functions in terms of its own inherent processes. Its raw materials are drawn from that special classification of events which both Freud and Jung, each in his own way, recognized as "psychic realities," the working facts of depth psychology.

The organic psyche has its own characteristics and its own principles of operation, but it is not separate from the body. The two rather compose a unity with the psychic part acting as the organ of guidance that directs the growth of the human being as a whole. The organic psyche is that aspect of the wholeness of the human organism that supplies the goals of man's activities and sets the direction of his development.

This role is performed in a variety of ways. The net effect of the functioning of the organic psyche is that it provides the human being with meanings for his life. But this, we should note, is not accomplished by a cerebral act. The meanings supplied by the organic psyche are not intellectual creations; nor can they be described as mainly feelings or emotions. Their essence is the image-making faculty of the psyche; they are products of imagination, but this is far from idle, irrelevant fantasying. The meanings that arise out of the organic psyche, often in symbolic forms, come rather from the very nature of the human organism, very much as the urge to build a nest arises out of the organic nature of the hummingbird.

In all species, what we speak of here as the *organic psyche* has been present and active as a silent guide within protoplasm, giving form to the organism and directing its efforts toward survival. When it arrives at the human level of the evolutionary process, it is able to become articulate; and with that step, what had only been implicit before becomes overt and tangible. The psyche demonstrates its presence in man by acting as the guiding and formative factor in his life. It had always functioned in this way in protoplasm; but at the level of evolution where the self-directiveness inherent in protoplasm takes human form it is able to make itself visible and vocal. From the silent guidance it gives to protoplasm in the simpler species, the psyche advances in man to the point where it can direct the life process by means of symbolic images, and eventually of words and concepts. At that point, it has come forth as a qualitatively new emergent in evolution.

The *organic psyche* represents something new, a culminating result of the evolutionary process of growth in the animal kingdom. And yet, in its principle of operation, it is the same as what it had always been.

The newness consists in the quality of consciousness that lifts human activities beyond the animal level. Man has the powers of discernment and judgment. He can choose this and reject that. He can value, cherish, exalt, and especially he can understand. The level of awareness of which the human psyche is capable represents a high achievement in the scale of evolution. It is a main instrument in the growth of civilization and in the development of the advanced capacities of consciousness that are the fulfillment of human personality.

The oldness, on the other hand, consists in the underlying instinctuality that is at the core of even the most advanced psychic activities. Man is pressed from behind to live out images of himself of which he is not even conscious. Yet he is impelled to do so. And the curious thing is that in striving to achieve his unconscious goals and to fulfill his unconscious motivations he behaves with high intelligence and awareness. When man, for example, finds himself driven by dark and obscure urges to go on a warpath, to tinker with new forms of technology, whether they be primitive flints or guided missiles, or when he undertakes the artist's search for beauty, a high degree of consciousness is expressed in his activity, even though the driving force behind the activity, the source of it, is not conscious at all.

This fact stands at the heart of the great paradox that has been both the challenge and the pitfall of psychologic study in the past. Man's life displays consciousness, and yet its roots are unconscious. If an interpretation of human personality is cast from the point of view either of consciousness or of the unconscious, it is bound to be one-sided. Its conceptions are almost inevitably weighted and colored by the aspect of the personality that it originally emphasized and took as its starting point. This has been a serious dilemma and frustration in the study of man in the past, wherever a psychological understanding has been attempted. And in particular it has presented a vexing problem to depth psychology, all the more so because of the variety and profundity of insights that have been reached through the concentrated study of the unconscious.

The holistic view of the *organic psyche,* which we have been describing here, opens the possibility of a new integral way of approach to the study of man. It is inherently a unitary conception, for its frame of reference is the life process itself. Its strength is that while its specific aim is to understand the psychologic quality of human experience, it avoids the misleading dichotomy between consciousness and the unconscious. The central fact in its approach to the study of man is the single seed of wholeness that is present as a potentiality in protoplasm, and grows toward fulfillment in the integral personality. The conception of the *organic psyche* thus gives us an integrative, affirmative perspective in which to study those forces in the human person that have previously been labeled the "unconscious."

In what forms does the *organic psyche* unfold the potentialities of its seed? To answer this, let us think of the example that Edmund Sinnott described, the hummingbird building her nest.

The bird spontaneously embarks upon a course of activity. There is no thought, no deliberation, preceding the act. It comes forth, naturally, of itself, impelled by large sums of instinctual energy (libido) that press for expression. This energy has a source that is deep in the nature of the organism. One can say that it is inherent in the protoplasmic structure of the bird. In other words, if the bird is to live out its life, if it is to survive as an individual and reach the maturity that is possible for its species, it will be necessary for this instinctual energy to be expressed. Otherwise the energy will regress into the organism and the life processes that are natural to the species will not be able to take place. The result will be confusion, disorientation, and finally the death of the organism.

We see then that the basic instinctual energies of the individual organism are virtually synonymous with its life. If these energies are dammed up for any reason, whether environmental or internal, the process of growth is seriously impeded, and eventually the survival of the creature is endangered.

The expression of life energies is essential, and it is, in fact, inherent in that basic principle in man of which we have spoken as the *survival drive*. The conversion of energy into activity is a vital necessity for the life and growth of the organism in every species. But, and this is an important qualification, in each case the instinctual life energies will express themselves only in those forms and in those directions that coincide with the image of activity built into the seed of its protoplasmic nature.

We may well speak of this as the *protoplasmic image*. It is the guiding image in the organism, the director and channelizer of its instinctual life energies. So, in the case of the hummingbird of which we were speaking, its basic survival drive was toward a preservation of life, and this included both its individual life and the life of its species. It was impelled to express its instinctual energies in terms of the survival form peculiar to its species, and this included procreation, nest-building, the bearing and nurturing of the young, all in accordance with a pattern of behavior that is present as an inborn tendency in all the members of its species. One could say that the bird has no choice. Its energies build up an inner tension as they accumulate within the organism, and they can be released in no other way. If the bird is to live and grow, it must be by means of this survival form, and with these particular hummingbird patterns of activity.

We realize, then, that the instinctual energies of the bird are actually inseparable from the forms in which they can be expressed. The protoplasmic nature of the bird does not provide raw, unformed energy that needs to be given a direction. The energy of protoplasm has its direction, even its ultimate goal, built into it, always in accordance with the form of its particular species.

It seems indeed that the problems presented by life for most species in the animal kingdom do not require them to find a direction for their energies. The direction and goals are given, and are taken for granted. Perhaps the sole exception to this is the human species in certain historical situations. In times of severe cultural transition like the present crisis in civilization, when basic beliefs about the nature of human existence have broken down, man finds himself without a clear conscious meaning for his life; and then his inner experience is of a surging of energy with no place to go. He seems at such moments to have lost the sense of direction that is inherent in his instincts. But that is not the usual situation in the animal kingdom. This most painful and precarious situation of energy with neither direction nor goal is reserved for the sovereign ruler of the animal kingdom, modern civilized man.

The direction in which energy is to be expressed and the pattern by which it is channelized are built into the guiding protoplasmic image of each species. In the typical situation in nature what is in question for the individual organism is not the form of his activities, for the form is given in the innate patterns of behavior, but what is in question is the particular object in which the activities shall be concretely embodied. Thus, for example, for the hummingbird there is no question of whether a nest is to be built; it is only a question of where and when and under what circumstances. It is a question, in other words, only of the particular nest.

With these observations in mind, we are in a position to perceive the pervading unity of the process of individual development. The guiding protoplasmic image that directs the growth of the seed of each organism is not only an image representing the goal of a pattern of behavior. It is an encompassing image in which there is implicit, in addition to the goal, the energy required for the activity, the outer objects upon which this energy is expressed in work, and the pattern of behavior which the individual organism carries out.

We see each of these aspects in the unity of action displayed in our hummingbird. Within the context of her species, she was enacting the *protoplasmic image* of the Mother. The goal in this case was the preservation of life. The energy was specifically sexual, but more generally instinctual; for, beginning with the immediate urge toward procreation, it extended into the elaborate preparations for nest-building and the subsequent nurture of the young. The outer objects embodying the process were the nest, the egg, the offspring. And the encompassing pattern of behavior in which all this was united in a single dynamic process was guided by the inarticulate image of the mother bird, which the organism blindly and beautifully enacted.

In this process, life was preserving and extending itself. But at the same time an individual organism was fulfilling its nature and was experiencing, relative to its level of consciousness, the supreme joy of living out the meaning of its life. In this sense the *protoplasmic images* of each of the species play a central role in the scheme of nature. They are the links by which the processes of life continue themselves. These guiding images, built into the protoplasmic core of the organism, draw life forward unknowingly, but with sure direction. The organism strives to do what its nature requires it to do; and to the degree that it succeeds in this, it connects itself to the ongoingness of the life process, helps to carry it forward, and is itself sustained by it.

The crucial element in this is the task that the protoplasmic image requires. This task is the goal that is implicit in the particular image. If it can be carried out, the image will be able to express itself concretely in the world; and in expressing itself, it will be able to grow and fulfill its possibilities. Otherwise, in disuse, it will atrophy and wither. In the hummingbird, the task of making ready for the offspring and taking care of it is the active core of its creative image. The baby hummingbirds are the art works of the species; and the nest-building and other tasks are the activities in which, and by which, the growth of the organism takes place.

THE MOVEMENT OF PROTOPLASMIC IMAGERY

The protoplasmic processes by which growth takes place in the simpler species are clear to us, at least in principle.

But what do we find at the human level? What is the protoplasmic imagery in man, and how does it operate?

The first difference that we notice is in the form in which the images are expressed. When we are discussing the lower species, the term "image" applies only metaphorically. The hummingbird does not have, as far as we can tell, an actual image of the nest and the egg and the offspring it will hatch. These are all parts of the process, but the process itself is blind. The animal is driven toward its goals by a dark instinctuality. It is prodded as though from behind, toward goals it does not see.

The human species, in contrast to this, does see its protoplasmic goals, even though they are presented to it in clouded and obscure forms. Man is able to see in his mind's eye visual images of the protoplasmic processes at work in him. He sees them in his dreams and in his fantasies, and it is undoubtedly true that some of the higher species possess this capacity as well, even if only in a rudimentary form.

Since these images are not products of man's conscious, rational understanding, they are not clear and straightforward in their meanings, but they are symbolic. Here, indeed, we come upon a basic explanation of the fact that the contents of the unconscious psyche are expressed in indirect, seemingly garbled symbolic forms. The reason is simply that the main frame of reference of the unconscious portions of the psyche is not found in the conscious attitudes of the individual, or even in his unconscious attitudes, even though many of the contents of the unconscious are the forgotten or repressed elements of previously conscious activities. Rather, the main frame of reference of the unconscious processes of the *organic psyche* is comprised of the goals and directions of life growth that are inherent in the protoplasmic organism. The individual is not and has never been conscious of them to more than a slight degree. Therefore, he experiences them in terms of the nonrationality of symbolism.

Another characteristic of protoplasmic imagery in man is that, although it is no more a function of consciousness than the flow of the blood stream is, it displays so high a degree of awareness in its instinctive activities that it often gives the illusion of seeming to be consciously self-directed. This quality of knowledge at the organic depth of the psyche involves a kind of unconscious knowing. It carries instinctive intimations and insights that are remarkably keen and perceptive.

The special quality of this type of cognition, however, is that it cannot be consciously or deliberately acquired. It is a kind of awareness that is valid only when it comes about spontaneously, when it "just happens." We have here one of the great paradoxes of human personality: the odd fact that one of the major sources of human knowledge, man's creative intuitions, cannot be reached by conscious intention because they are dependent upon the nonconscious workings of the organic psyche. Nonetheless, the insights into the dynamic processes of the psyche which depth psychology brings make it possible to devise methods of channeling these processes in the direction of creative work. We shall see a significant aspect of this a little later on when we discuss the psychology of scientific discovery.[1]

The psyche of man is always full of images in a great variety of forms, ranging from highly conscious clarity to a blurred obscurity of meaning. These images are highly fluid and variable. There seems to be taking place at the several subliminal levels of the psyche a constant flow of imagery. Included in this are mental images, symbolic representations, metaphoric figures, pictures, ideas, and concepts. All these participate in a continuous flow of imagery that underlies the productions of consciousness.

This flow of imagery may force itself to the forefront of awareness now and again in dreams, in fantasies and reveries, as well as in conscious thinking. But always there is vastly more that does not reveal itself. It is as though there were large schools of fish swimming at various depths below the surface of the ocean, and occasionally a few individual fish pop their heads into the open air and permit themselves to be seen. This would be a very small number in relation to the total number of fish swimming about underneath. But it would be a significant revelation in that it would disclose the kind of fish swimming in the area. One of the useful functions of dreams is that they do something similar. They have no meaning statistically, but dreams can give us a revealing, though admittedly partial, glimpse of the general tenor of what is taking place beneath the surface.

[1] See Chapter IX.

Whatever its specific contents are, the general characteristic of what is below the surface of the psyche is that
it is *a flow of imagery*. We can verify this easily by merely
checking ourselves in the midst of a reverie. The images
have been moving forward within us under their own
momentum, undirected, and in a steady flow. Likewise,
if we pause in our conscious activities, and imagine a
kind of movie screen before our mind's eye, we will soon
see a stream of images form and move one by one upon
the screen. This takes very little practice and can be
developed in a number of ways to achieve a wide variety
of purposes, some of which we shall discuss in a later
section of this book.

The imagery of the psyche is constantly in movement.
Or, another way to describe it is that the processes of the
psyche are expressed in imagery. *Imagery in movement
is the essence of the psyche* and of all the processes by
which it reaches fulfillment.

Imagery is in movement constantly at all levels of the
psyche. It is in flow on the one hand at levels that are
close to consciousness and from which it may be easily
translated into rational terms. And it is in flow also at
deeper basic levels, where the symbolism is much more
obscure and its immediate relation to the environment
is slim indeed. Imagery moves on all the various levels of
the psyche and in a variety of forms, but there is an encompassing, unifying principle directing the flow. This
principle is the essence of the individuality of each organic
psyche. It is the one integrating principle working to-

ward the wholeness of the person; and all the separate and segmental psychic processes draw their guiding pattern from it.

It is as though a tulip bulb, with the style and color of its flower already contained implicitly within it, grew toward the unfoldment of this flower by a process in which images followed one upon the other until the ultimate image contained originally in the bulb was fulfilled. What was present as potentiality at the very outset acts as the pervading and unifying principle throughout the life of the organism. When the growth process deviates from this centralizing principle, it is stymied until the split is healed. The individual must be returned to himself in order to grow integrally; and this is another way of saying that growth is possible only when it is in accord with the image present in the seed of the organism.

The movement of imagery in the psyche reflects the degree of this accord or the absence of it. The patterns of image formation disclose whether the psyche is moving toward wholeness or whether it has been sidetracked into self-segmentation. In this regard, dreams are a particularly significant token of the situation of the personality as a whole. Certain dreams, especially those that are brought forth in a moment of great tension, reflect the condition of the psyche as a unity, the situation of the dreamer, the style and pattern of his psychic processes, and the deep unconscious direction that his life is taking, whether it is fulfilling the seed-image of his personality or is moving fruitlessly away from it.

Such dreams are especially meaningful instances of

the flow of protoplasmic imagery. They are part of the constant creation and movement of images that is ever taking place in the psyche on all its levels. Such imagery is always present in the psyche, is always moving about, enlarging, relating, transforming, symbolizing itself. But in the tension of a great crisis in the individual's life the regular, unceasing flow of imagery is stimulated, intensified, deepened, and at the same time brought closer to the surface. It is then that one has dreams that derive from the deepest recesses of the psyche, drawing material from the darkest corners of the self in its historic, cosmic, transpersonal aspects; and yet, deep though they are, and distant though their sources may be, they come vividly to the mind and establish themselves in the consciousness of the individual as *realities* of his experience that he can never erase from his life even though he knows they are "only dreams." The dream of the luminous child, which we described in an earlier chapter, is a good instance of this. It was a dream that came at a moment of tension in which the fullness of the psyche and all its possibilities were brought to the fore in the most direct and eloquent way. Another dream of this kind, though somewhat less spiritual but nonetheless dramatic and transforming, was the dream of killing Siegfried that came to C. G. Jung in 1913.[2]

Jung dreamt that dream at the time that he was en-

2 For a description and close discussion of that dream and its significance for the history of depth psychology, see Ira Progoff, *The Death and Rebirth of Psychology*, New York, Julian Press, 1956, Chap. IV, Sec. 3, "The Deepening of Jung's Personal Perspective," pp. 119-133.

gaged in breaking his connection with the psychoanalytic movement and venturing to define his own conceptions in depth psychology. It was a time of tension and of great uncertainty in his life, and this tension brought to the fore images of deep historic significance and of a power much greater than his merely personal memories and wishes. Likewise, coming at a time of crisis and of determined but fearful decision, it described not only a crossroad in life but a crossroad in the psyche. It therefore set forth the essential pattern of growth in Jung's life that was to follow in subsequent years. Dreams of that kind are exceedingly vivid, but their dark symbolism is difficult to decipher. When they are penetrated and understood, however, they reveal not only the style of the psyche in the past but the way in which it will bear itself in the future. They are, therefore, dreams that not only carry an intense feeling of reality but also a substantial hint of prediction drawn from the depths of the psyche.

The flow of protoplasmic imagery crystallizes its meaning and direction in such dreams that appear in moments of crisis; but imagery that is the same in principle, expressing the same essential content and dramatizing itself in the same style, appears also in many other forms. It appears in much simpler dreams that are not nearly as deep and not as vividly experienced. It comes in daydreams, in reveries, in the invoking of fantasies for poetic and other inspiration, in prayer, in art works, in doodling, even in thinking.

These are the quiet forms, the more psychological forms in which imagery is expressed. But the imagery of the deep psyche is also *directly lived out in the enactment of life,* and this active aspect has a very great and often unappreciated importance in the growth of personality.

The movement of imagery in dreams, in doodling, and in inspirations has a visual form that can be perceived. The visual forms behind thought processes, expressing the pattern of an image, can also be perceived, at least in principle. But activities that are not dreamed but are enacted directly in life seem not to have an image behind them. Thus it is that the man of spontaneous action, whether he be engaged in car racing or in business competition, feels that there is nothing psychological in his work. He is not aware of the image deep in his psyche directing and shaping the pattern of his activities.

Only when his activities reach a stalemate in life, so that the energy dams up and the image cannot be directly enacted in life, is there an opportunity for the man of outer action to realize the psychological forces that have been guiding his behavior. Energy that cannot go outward in activity often expresses itself in dreams, and then the imagery that has always been in the background can be seen. The dream images depicting the frustrated adventurer, in whatever field of activity his adventures have been cast, will demonstrate that the image of the adventurer has indeed been there attempting to be the formative factor in the individual's life.

EMERGENT INDIVIDUALITY

How do these principles of personality growth work themselves out in the life of the individual?

A child is born into a world he did not choose. He does not choose the time, the place, and most important, he does not choose his parents. Neither does he choose his body, but the organism that is his is his own nature and his life. That is given, the "he" that is his specific being, the raw and prime material of his existence.

Why does the child not choose these things? Because his individuality has not yet been formed? Much better to say because the specific formative principle, the seed of his individuality, has not yet appeared, has not yet disclosed itself nor indicated the stamp that its nature will place upon events.

As the child grows, he absorbs the feelings and conceptions of his parents, his teachers, his neighbors, and all the other persons who comprise the environment of his young life. He finds himself in relationships with them, and their more developed individualities set the tone of the relationships. Thus the child may be caught in a very strong tie to one of the parents, reacting to a need of the parents, much more than to a need of his own. He may find himself unconsciously driven to express the libido that one of his parents could never express in his own life, whether this is sexual libido or psychic energy that has been frustrated in finding its channel for work. We all know of the young men who drive ahead toward professions their parents dreamed of, but who do not pause to discover the special seed of personality that is trying to grow in them. They must ultimately retrace their steps in order to find themselves. And we know also the young man who feels "called" to enter the church, but who has actually heard not the inner voice within him but the unfulfilled spirituality of one of his parents.

In a host of forms, the child absorbs the feelings, the thoughts, the patterns of belief, and the styles of reaction to life that are expressed by his parents, and by those with whom he comes into close and repeated contact. We know of many cases in which a child's dream was more expressive of his parent's psychic life than of his own. And this is only an indication of how close the unconscious identification of the child with an adult may become. It takes place in forms that are much less obvious but which nonetheless pervade the inner tissue of character and behavior of the child.

In the course of his activities and participation in the world around him, the child develops a particular "style of life." Alfred Adler tells us that this is more or less fixed in its basic characteristics by the time the child is five years of age. This "style" is a kind of "psychic gait" in Adler's phrase, and it reflects the way in which the individual is unconsciously thinking of himself. But close sociological analysis in this regard, especially the brilliant work of George Herbert Mead,[3] has indicated that the way in which the child thinks of himself is in large part derived from the way in which others think of him. The

[3] See *Mind, Self, and Society*, Chicago, University of Chicago Press, 1934.

child takes over the attitude of the other person toward himself, and thinks of himself as others think of him. And much more important, he *acts* in accordance with the way other people think of him. He thus builds up his style of life not out of his own indigenous nature, but out of the attitudes of other persons in his environment, the most important of whom are usually the parents. This *familial* or *environmental self* expresses the main pattern and characteristics of the child as a socially conditioned being; and not of the child alone, but in most cases of the adult as well.

The question then must be asked, Where is the individual? He has come into a world he did not choose, into a situation he did not choose, and now he finds himself living out an image of life and even of his own personality that is not his own, but is derived from other persons. Where indeed is his own individuality and from what source does it appear? The insights we drew from the works of Jan Christian Smuts and especially of Edmund Sinnott provide a perspective in which we can answer this question.

Each individual human being is an organism; in the sense of Smuts, it is a *whole*. But wholeness in this framework of thinking has a twofold meaning. It is fulfillment, the ultimate outcome, the meaning and goal, of a long process; and it is also potentiality working toward fulfillment. Wholeness is present in essence in the seed of the individual, but it becomes an actuality only gradually as the process unfolds.

But where does the process begin? What are its sources? Its sources are within the seed of the organism, as the tulip grows from its bulb. The environment may hinder it or help it, may bend it or distort it, but nothing else than a tulip can grow from the bulb. This is because the essence of the seed is fixed at the beginning, and wholeness for the tulip is the fulfillment of what is present as potentiality in the seed of the organism. But always, and this is especially true of the feeling of personal experience in the human being, potentiality fulfills itself gradually in a process that is growth, but growth unperceived by the individual himself until after it has taken place. The process of growth moves forward bit by bit. It moves forward toward the ultimate image of fulfillment that is deep in the core of the seed of each human individual. But truly that image is far in the background, and off in the wings of the future. It is working actively in the process of unfoldment, but unseen like a guardian angel who remains hidden while he does his deeds of guidance.

What the individual does see instead of the ultimate image are the specific goals, the specific desires and ambitions that represent the aims of activity at various points along the road of his life. These may reflect the age of the person. The goals of the adolescent are not the same as those of the man of forty, but they somehow lead to them, even by indirection. Or, equally, these goals may reflect the stage of personal development that has been achieved out of the life experience of the person. But always and inevitably these goals are cast in terms of an image, for an image is necessary in principle to present the meaning of the activity in a form that can work in the deep psyche and draw its energies forward.

Now the question is, whose images are these that are providing the goals and directions of the individual's life activities? In the vast majority of cases, they are not the individual's own images. They are not derived from the deep psyche of the person himself, but they derive rather from his contact with his family and his environment in general. They are images that he has drawn not from the seed deep in his nature, but from the attitudes of other persons, attitudes that he has absorbed as though they were his own. This is true of the obedient child who fulfills the desires of his parents. It is true also of the child who feels that people's image of him is as an outsider and he, absorbing this image of himself as though it were his own, enacts the image of the disobedient one.

These images of the *environmental self* are effective within the personality. They act to draw forth psychic energy and to bring the individual into the vortex of events in his social world. But they are not images that are drawn from the treasure house of his own psyche. They may be excellent images. They may work very well in making a comfortable life possible for him, but they are not his own images. They are someone else's. They are society's images of him.

Is it then important that the person express his own inherent image in the development of his personality in life? May he not be happy without it, simply living out an image he has derived from society or from his family, an image he has adopted as his own? He may indeed be happy this way. But he also may not.

Think of the father who wished to be a doctor but was frustrated in his desire and had to settle for a profession he did not value as highly. He presses his son to fulfill the ambition he himself did not achieve until the adolescent boy seems "spontaneously" to think of himself as becoming a doctor. A similar result may come about where the father is a doctor, or a fireman, and the son spontaneously desires to "be like his daddy." This boyish phrase, translated into our frame of reference, means simply that the young man wants to live out the same life image as his father, without waiting to discover what his own indigenous image is.

In either of these situations, the boy may use his native intellect to carry him through the studies that are required for the medical degree, only to find then that his work in his "chosen" profession in some vague way makes him feel uneasy. He finds himself ridden by anxieties that he cannot explain. His psychic equilibrium is upset, and he is disturbed by dreams he cannot understand. These dreams, however, or their equivalent in deep fantasy, will very probably divulge the secret of the young man's problem. This is because the flow of imagery that is inherent in the organic psyche expresses itself in dreams, or in their equivalent in fantasy material. Hidden in the flow of protoplasmic imagery that will thus come through in symbolic form will be the image that is seeking to emerge in the young man's life, the image that his nature requires him to fulfill.

Now a painful process will have forced itself upon the young man. Perhaps the image pressing him from within requires that he concern himself with art, or with business, or with carpentry—no matter what. The important thing is that it will have brought him into contact with an image that derives from his own psyche and not from the psyche of another person. It will not be an ersatz that he has taken over unknowingly from other persons, whether a parent, a teacher, or the anonymous opinions of society in a conformist's world. Now he will have learned that a person cannot grow unless he is rooted in his own inherent nature. He will then have to set about the difficult but eventually very satisfying task of rearranging his life so that he will be able to live in contact with the seed of his own being, enacting in the world an image that is organically his own insofar as it has come to him from the depths of his own psyche.

DEPOSING THE ENVIRONMENTAL SELF

But now let us consider the case of an individual in whom nothing went seriously wrong, no anxieties, no malaise, no disturbing dreams. How would the growth of individuality take place here?

In the early years of the child's life, a self and a style of life would develop in terms that we have described, derived from the close contact with other individuals in the family and the social environment as a whole. This would be the *environmental self.* It would not be the individual's *real* nature, for that *real* nature would not yet have disclosed itself. But it would be the self that carried his name in society, that bore the qualities that others ascribed to him, and that eventually described the way in which he thought of himself.

This would characterize the early years of childhood, but some years later—perhaps in the early teens, although the specific age seems to vary considerably—an image indicating the inner, intrinsic tendency of the individual would emerge. It would not show itself clearly, nor in a strong form; for it would be young, weak, and therefore hesitant. It would disclose itself, however, in a new and consistent expression of energy in some particular channel. It might be writing, business, music, a girl's interest in the home. If it were an image that required some specific talent or training, its expression might well be premature, and then its growth would depend a great deal upon its receiving outside encouragement.

Ultimately, however, the environment is not the deciding factor where the emergent image is concerned. It depends upon itself, and especially upon the degree of energy with which it finds itself thrust forth from the organic psyche. Now let us assume that the amount of energy available to the emergent image is large. It is thus able to move forward strongly in the individual to find its place in his life and to become the central image that he will enact in his existence. Let us also assume, as we have said, that it is not a case in which the individual has embarked upon a course of activity based upon a derived familial image. The individual's own essential image is coming forth. Now what can we expect to happen?

Circumstances vary, but one set of psychic events seems to be inevitable. There will be in some form an inner conflict between the image of himself which the young person had cast in terms of his environment and the image emerging under its own power from the depth of the organic psyche. This is an *inner* conflict, but it is inevitably projected outward. The individual will see it as a struggle against authority, against specific authorities, against society in general, against specific cultures and folkways, or against the father or the mother. These are all projections and symbolizations of a conflict that is taking place within the personality. It is a conflict between the style of life that characterized the image of the *environmental self,* which the person had derived as a child from those around him, and the emergent image that would now aspire to make him an individual in his own right.

This is indeed a difficult conflict to endure. It involves the death of a part of the personality, the old part to which one had grown accustomed in childhood. To overcome this part of the self is very much like a murder, as it has been described in psychoanalytic theory. It is, indeed, a killing of that part of the personality that is associated with the family. In Freud's personal situation, since he had grown up in a severely patriarchal family situation, it was just natural that he identify the family image with the father. The overcoming of the familial image in order to make way for the emergent image of personality was therefore symbolized in his dreams as a killing of the father. But Freud mistook that for a wish to kill his actual father, not realizing that the father, as a representative of authority, is a natural symbol for the environmental self which must be replaced if a mature and creative personality is to grow. When one considers it, it seems that the entire Oedipus theory, the complex named for it, and the damage that has been done by the emphasis upon personal conflict between parent and child, are all derived from this simple but natural error in Freud's thinking.

The conflict that takes place *within* the personality is, however, very real and painful, for the habits of the environmental self are deeply engraved as patterns of behavior in the individual psyche. They are not easily replaced. And yet they must be replaced if the new image is to take a dominant and guiding role in the individual's growth. The result of this can be a tension of almost unbearable intensity, so painful that the eventual answer is usually a compromise in which some elements of the old self remain in the personality as mementos of the past while new creative patterns of development emerge as well. To the observer this gives the impression of a seesawing in the personality as the old and new intermingle throughout the life of the growing personality. It is difficult to find an example of a well-developed person who is not in some significant degree subject to this rule.

This discussion of the early self of childhood and the emergent self of individuality makes it possible to understand and appreciate certain basic conceptions of psychoanalysis in a larger perspective. The studies of infancy and early childhood to which Freudian psychoanalysis has devoted so much attention turn out, in the present context, to be a detailed analysis of how the environmental self with its familial images comes into being. It does not concern the emergent images that carry the specific individuality of the person and provide the directing creative force in personal growth.

This is a most significant point because it enables us to see what Freud was doing and to understand why he was forced to acknowledge the limitations of his psychoanalytic concepts where creative acts of personality were concerned. One recalls in this regard his fascinating and classic attempt to interpret the smile of the Mona Lisa in terms of the childhood experiences of Leonardo. At the end of his study, Freud, ever the honest man, had to say, "we have to admit that the nature of artistic attainment is psychoanalytically inaccessible to us." [4]

We may add the comment that the reason that the nature of creativity is inaccessible to psychoanalysis is that its main concepts as well as its method of approach are directed toward the study of the *environmental self*. This is specifically that part of the personality that *precedes* the emergence of the creative image of individuality. In fact, it disappears to the degree that a creative image comes forth and is able to establish its position.

It seems correct to say, therefore, that the part of the psyche upon which psychoanalysis concentrates its attention is specifically the *noncreative* part. This is neces-

[4] Sigmund Freud, *Leonardo da Vinci, A Study in Psychosexuality*, New York, Modern Library, p. 119.

sarily so, since psychoanalysis was designed as a theory of neurosis constructed from a medical point of view. Attempts to pretend that psychoanalysis contains a theory of creativity merely confuses the issues. It would be much wiser to accept the fact that psychoanalysis is intended to be nothing more than a means of interpreting and analyzing neurosis. Once we recognize the deliberate self-imposed limitation on Freud's work, we are free to find a set of conceptions capable of providing an entrée into the creative depths of personality.

A main criterion for such a framework of concepts would be its ability to interpret the fact that the active principle working in the human organism is an image guiding the growth of personality and providing the basis for the entire functioning of the psyche. The basis for such an understanding is to be found in the unitary biology of Edmund Sinnott. With it, and interpreting the depths of personality in holistic terms, we are able to work out a way toward the two ultimate purposes that a psychology must serve if it is to meet the needs of modern man. These are, firstly, to understand and describe the processes by which the integral personality emerges in principle through the creative unfoldment of images in the organic psyche; and secondly, to devise practical procedures by which the development of holistic personality can be heightened and expedited.

THE DYNATYPES AND THE COGNITYPES

It is time now for us to return to the fuller perspective of thought, which we have been marking off in this volume as a means of studying the processes of the organic psyche. We have seen the role that the psyche plays in the scheme of nature. It is the directive part of the organism, the part that supplies its goals and the inner meanings of its activities. Ultimately the goal of the psyche is life, specifically the life of the individual organism. More generally, it is the life of the species, and more abstractly still but no less real, it is the extension of life in itself. This takes many forms, as we have seen in an earlier section, so that *qualitative survival,* which is the extension of life in terms of meaning, becomes ultimately the psyche's main though unconscious criterion as it functions in modern civilization.

The psyche works for life qualitatively in terms of meaning, and these meanings are brought forth out of the psyche itself in the form of images. In lower animal species these images are implicit and are revealed only in overt activities, as the beaver builds the dam or the bees maintain their hive. But in man they take a definite and knowable form, for they are visual and even verbal so that they can be articulated. Imagery does become available for use in thinking in man, but the imagery that works in the depths of the psyche to guide the psyche spontaneously in the direction of life does not operate on a conscious level. In one sense it is much more primal,

more instinctual; in another sense it is much more fundamental, more profound. These are some of the special
qualities of the contents of the deep psyche, and they
need to be remembered when we undertake to work with
them in practical applications.

The organic psyche is best understood as a continuous
process. There is an ongoing flow of imagery taking place
all the time, a very small part of which comes close
enough to consciousness for us to become aware of it. This
flow of protoplasmic imagery expresses and works toward
the realization of a central image, an image that is for the
human species what the image of nest-building and life-
preservation is for the hummingbird. It is an image that
expresses the seed of the species, the protoplasmic nature
of the organism. It contains the essence in potentiality of
what the human being can do, and what the human being
can become. The fulfillment of this is wholeness. It
brings what Smuts spoke of as *holistic personality.*

Wholeness is an image expressing the essence of the
psyche, the integral nature of personality. It is present,
in principle, and the way it takes form in actuality is
as a flow of imagery that moves toward the fulfillment of
the image of wholeness. This imagery comprises the contents of the organic psyche. It is what the psyche is in
operation.

Many of the contents of the psyche are drawn from
conscious experience, either as remnants and memories
of past events or as wishful aspirations for the future. But
where this is the case they represent only a superficial part
of the psyche. The truly important and dynamic, the

creating part of the psyche, is not derived from the environment. It comes rather from the inherent nature of the individual organism. These are the images that express the protoplasmic goals of the human being. Or, another way to describe it is that these fundamental images provide the specific patterns with which the encompassing image of wholeness works toward fulfillment.

The patterns of imagery in the organic psyche are basically of two kinds: The *enacting images,* or *dynatypes,* and the *formative images,* or *cognitypes.*

The *dynatypes* are the images that provide the directive patterns of behavior for specific styles of individual development. These contain within the seed of personality the dynamic principles by which each type of individual grows toward maturity and toward the fulfillment of the potentialities inherent in his particular nature.

The dynatypes correspond to the images that provide the spontaneous, instinctive direction for the behavior of animal species; but they have one important difference. In each animal species there is a single style of activity that is possible for it; a squirrel can behave only as a squirrel, and in no other way; squirrelness does not encompass significant variations. By contrast, however, the human species is exceedingly complicated. A very large variety of styles of behavior is possible for man. That has a great deal to do with the advanced developments of civilization; but in some way that we have yet to discover, the underlying patterns of civilized behavior are carried in the structure of the organic psyche as seeds of potentiality, as *tendencies* toward specific styles of activity. This does not necessarily imply the inheritance of acquired characteristics, although something comparable may in fact be taking place. What it does imply is that, as a result of the close relationship between the functioning of the psyche in man and the inherent sociality of human nature, marked proclivities toward specific styles of social behavior become fixed in the psyche and assert themselves in terms of the patterns and flow of imagery that are characteristic of the organic psyche.

There is a great deal of study and discussion of the dynatypes that can contribute to an understanding of the struggle for wholeness in the modern personality. We must reserve that discussion for another place and context. Our purpose here is mainly to distinguish the dynatypes as a specific class of imagery working in the organic psyche, and to indicate the principles by which they function.

The dynatypes act themselves out; they dramatize themselves in life. They are images in the sense of the guiding meaning directing particular styles of behavior; they represent and lead to patterns of behavior in terms of civilized life. Thus we have the dynatype of the Adventurer, for the Adventurer fulfills always a particular pattern of life whether his adventuring is in the business world, the hunt, brigandage, or athletics. There is the dynatype of the prophet who speaks of social reality in a name higher than his own; and closely related to this is the political leader of the charismatic type, the leader who inspires his followers and who states his political doctrines in a religious or philosophical frame of reference. We might remark parenthetically here that what Max Weber spoke of as *charisma* in leadership is essentially the degree of intensity with which the dynatypal image is enacted.

There is the dynatype of the seer and the dream interpreter, a figure whose prototype is Joseph in the Bible, and which Sigmund Freud re-enacted in recent times. There is the dynatype of the teacher, a figure that is expressed in a wide variety of forms such as the master, the guru, the rabbi, the wise old man. Corresponding to this, there is the dynatype of the seeker for truth in various forms. The seeker for truth in nature is expressed in modern times as the scientist, and in earlier times as the astrologer and alchemist. The seeker for truth in God may be the disciple or the wanderer, for he has many forms in human history, many variations upon the central theme of his life.

The number of dynatypes is large, and the task of identifying the characteristics of the individual dynatypes still lies before us. From the practical point of view of drawing forth the greatest creative potential in modern individuals, what is most important is not, however, the analysis of the dynatypes but the process by which they express themselves in life. In fact, the essence of the dynatypes is really anti-analytical. Their nature is to move forward, to grow as they express themselves in outward works. The dynatypes require an opus in which to be engaged, so that, as they enact themselves, the capacities implicit in their seed come forth and unfold toward the maturity of the organism. This is a very important quality of the dynatypes, for it expresses a basic principle in the operation of the organic psyche. We shall have occasion to look at it more closely a little later on.

The second classification of protoplasmic imagery which we have mentioned, the *formative images* or *cognitypes,* provide the underlying patterns in which the human being apprehends reality. These are the basic forms of thought, the images within the structure of the organic psyche which set both the limits and the possibilities for man's knowledge. These images present the primary categories in which all the varieties of knowledge, conjecture, and belief are formed and are felt within the psyche. They provide the basic types of human cognition, whether in terms of intellect, intuition, feeling, or any other medium. Thus the term, *cognitype.*

The cognitypes are formative images in the sense that raw, unclassified observations are given shape and meaning by them. This is not only for intellectual knowledge but for religious types of experience as well. Thus the cognitype of energy may be experienced as soul-force or mana in a primitive or animistic view of the world, whereas it will have a mechanical meaning or an abstract mathematical meaning in the modern world. Likewise the cognitype of the atom appears in Hindu mythology as the world egg, in European philosophy as the monad, again as the image of the microcosm-macrocosm relationship, and ultimately in the modern theory of atoms and molecules.

There is a very large and illuminating work of research and correlation waiting to be done in identifying and describing the unifying patterns in the psyche that underlie the basic categories of knowledge. Such authors as F. M. Cornford, Henri Frankfort, C. G. Jung, Mircea Eliade, and Pitirim Sorokin have already made very impressive contributions in this direction, working from diverse points of view. The identification of the various cognitypes is, however, not of primary concern in our present context. It lies beyond the immediate purposes of this book, at a further stage in the development of depth psychology as an integrating tool in the study of man. There, the interpretation of the cognitypes in terms of the depth processes of the organic psyche will one day make a large contribution to the holistic study of culture and will illuminate the history of philosophy and science. Here, however, our interest is not to analyze the details of the cognitypes but simply to point out that this is one of the two basic classifications of protoplasmic imagery in the organic psyche. We shall have an opportunity to see the practical importance of the cognitypes in the life of modern man a little later in our discussion.

8 * *Imagery in personal growth*

In whatever form we understand it, and regardless of the nomenclature with which we interpret it, it is essential that we grasp the implications of the fundamental insight that the human personality unfolds by means of images. This is a basic fact. Much more, it is a basic experience. It reaches beyond special concepts, and this is perhaps the reason that in recent years it has been emphasized by a variety of authors whose viewpoints otherwise diverge widely from one another.

Among the most significant of these is the Norton Lectures delivered at Harvard in 1953/54 by Sir Herbert

Read. These lectures, published under the title, *Icon and Idea*,[1] are an attempt to interpret man's "image-making faculty" in relation to the development of art and civilization in general. Read's central theme and his conclusions derive from his underlying view that the source of man's conceptions of reality is not the intellect but the nonrational depths of the psyche; for it is there that symbols are made.

Thinking in these terms, Read comes to the question of which came first, the image or the idea, the artist or the philosopher. This is not an idle replay of the old riddle concerning the chicken and the egg. It concerns a central principle in the operation of the organic psyche.

The question at issue is not necessarily which comes first chronologically. It is a question of which factors come first *in principle*. Thus, in Read's understanding of it, there is first the icon, the image represented in a work of art; and following upon that, there is the work of the philosopher who draws forth the meaning, the intellectual ideas about reality that are implicit in the form and flavor of the icon.

That is the order of events seen from the point of view of the history of culture. And its equivalent, seen from the point of view of depth psychology in the perspective of the organic psyche, is that first there is the protoplasmic imagery that comes forth autonomically, nonconsciously, and in nonrational forms, veiled and symbolic. Then there comes the conscious extrapolation of meanings from

[1] Sir Herbert Read, *Icon and Idea, The Function of Art in the Development of Human Consciousness,* Cambridge, Harvard University Press, 1955.

the image and their elaboration into ideas and concepts. From this comes man's philosophies of life and his sciences of life. They are derivatives of the primary imagery of the psyche.

The varieties of protoplasmic imagery are pregnant with meanings and with implications as to the nature of man, his existence, and the universe in which he grows. But the images themselves do not "know" these meanings; they only express them. They only reveal them, and it is left for the steadily emerging consciousness of man, the steadily sharpening intellect of the individual, to draw forth and delineate the intuitive knowledge revealed in the images. So, in comparable terms, the artist does not consciously know the fullness of what he is disclosing in the imagery of his art work. He simply places a form there; and the interpreter of art, the man of intellect and of a kind of intuition other than the artist's, comes and finds material in the natural symbolism of the art work with which to construct his philosophies.

Because he thinks of the production of imagery as the primary activity of the psyche, Sir Herbert is able to perceive in the history of art the unfoldment of man's creativity and the foundations of his consciousness. Art is then, in such a framework, not merely a specialized product of a sophisticated culture; it is the stuff of life. It is the expression of the holistic process inherent in the human organism by which its protoplasmic nature brings forth the imagery of life; and by which it is raised slowly and marvelously to consciousness.

Since art, in this understanding of it, expresses the

generic qualities of the human psyche as these are experienced in any given period of history, it cannot truly be thought of as the work of a comparatively few talented individuals. The talented ones, the geniuses, are the artists who are most sensitive to the imagery that is present and moving in the dark, nonpersonal recesses of their own psyche, and that is active in the psychic depths of their contemporaries as well. Thus they bring to expression what is working not only in themselves but in their fellow men as well.

What they do in their art constitutes an organic act. It is biologic; it is psychologic; it is social. Read indicates all this very well when he remarks toward the close of his discussion, "The history of art and the development of human consciousness are biological processes which we can best study and promote as activities rather than as classified documents." [2] The process by which the image-making faculty of man unfolds and fulfills itself is central in the life of the psyche and in human development as a whole; and Read conceives of art in this sense as the cultural embodiment of the first and basic phase of the process by which the psyche unfolds.

It is, I think, of more than passing significance to note that Read's theme is in close accord with the underlying conception of the unconscious as developed by both Freud and Jung. It touches something that is fundamental in depth psychology as a whole, and thus it reaches beyond particular points of view. The primacy of imagery is inherent in Freud's original insight into the nature of the

[2] *Ibid.*, p. 137.

unconscious, and it remained an important part of his thinking. Thus, in *The Ego and the Id*, a major work of his mature years, Freud wrote, "Thinking in picture . . . approximates more closely to unconscious processes than thinking in words, and it is unquestionably older than the latter both ontogenetically and phylogenetically." [3]

A statement of this kind represents the side of Freud's thinking that was extended by C. G. Jung in developing his theory of the "Archetypes of the Collective Unconscious." Jung understood by the archetypes the underlying patterns of imagery at the depths of the psyche, and drawing upon Freud's descriptions, he interpreted such images as being more fundamental than thoughts and words. Conscious thoughts are ultimately derived from the archetypal images. They emerge from them by a process of what Jung called "differentiation." Thinking separates itself from the unconscious expression of the images, and thus ideas are born. This again corresponds to the general order of events as Read describes them, paralleling Jung's recurrent phrase, "Consciousness comes from the unconscious."

One advantage of Read's way of approaching his subject matter is that it enables him to bridge the somewhat artificial dichotomy of consciousness and the unconscious in man. In this regard, his work corresponds most closely to the perspective we have been establishing in these pages. Here, while interpreting what has been spoken of as consciousness and the unconscious, we have emphasized the

[3] Sigmund Freud, *The Ego and the Id*, p. 23.

unitary quality of the human personality. Thus we set the organic psyche as our holistic context in the study of man, recognizing the organic psyche to be the organ of meaning and of qualitative survival in man, in which and by which the emergent goals of man's protoplasmic nature move toward fulfillment.

In relation to this perspective, Read's inferences from the study of art and other cultural artifacts supply considerable data that amplify our understanding of what protoplasmic imagery contains. These inferences also open the rewarding possibility that the further investigation of art in the depth perspective of the organic psyche will bring us into ever closer contact with the creative processes in human nature.

THE SCIENTIST AS ARTIST: THE OBSERVATIONS OF JACOB BRONOWSKI

Another most significant insight into the role of images in human activity was recently presented by the eminent mathematician and interpreter of William Blake, Jacob Bronowski, in his book, *Science and Human Values.*[4] Professor Bronowski is author of the classic report on "The Effects of the Atomic Bombs at Hiroshima and Nagasaki," written for the British Chiefs of Staff; and he also directs research for the National Coal Board in Great

[4] Jacob Bronowski, *Science and Human Values,* New York, Julian Messner, 1956.

Britain. His life is a most unusual combination of abstract theorizing, poetic sensitivity, relatedness to historical realities, and concern with practical affairs. It is a most impressive array, and it seems indeed that this combination of interests and activities has placed Bronowski in a position to have particularly penetrating insights into the psychology of creative persons.

Bronowski makes some observations of the largest implications on the relation between science and art by calling attention to correspondences that have seldom been recognized. He speaks of the creative artist in the field of poetry and painting; and he speaks of the creative scientist, the man who works with the "facts" until a new view of them becomes possible. And then, raising the question of whether these two types of persons are really as different as they are generally thought to be, he calls attention to an underlying sameness in their mentality. They are both expressing in their lives what he calls "the creative mind." But what does this involve?

Modern science, as it was growing and building its reputation for empiric objectivity, constantly emphasized that it was dealing "only with the facts." It spoke of its work as "morally colorless"; and it described its point of view as "the dry light of science." [5] But this has given a very misleading impression of what the work of scientific discovery actually entails. Whenever a basic discovery has been made, the essential facts have been available for some time for all the specialists in the field to see; and yet no

[5] See Thorstein Veblen, *The Place of Science in Modern Civilization,* New York, Viking, 1942.

new discovery has resulted until some special psychic event took place. What then is the special psychologic quality of scientific discovery?

Bronowski looks at the work of Copernicus for a clue to the essential ingredient, the factor that makes the difference. Copernicus, he says, had come upon a new view of things that seemed to him more workable. He "found that the orbits of the planets would look simpler if they were looked at from the sun and not from the earth." But how had Copernicus reached this conclusion? By observing the same facts as everyone else? By following the routine procedures of arithmetic to calculate this and that in all their possibilities? No. Where Copernicus was concerned, Bronowski writes, "His first step was a leap of imagination—to lift himself from the earth, and put himself wildly, speculatively into the sun. 'The earth conceives from the sun,' he wrote; and 'the sun rules the family of stars.' We catch in his mind an image, the gesture of the virile man standing in the sun, with arms outstretched, overlooking the planets." [6]

Now let us ask, what is implied in this *image*, and what can we learn from it about the creative nature of the psyche when we consider it in terms of the conceptions of depth psychology, which we have been discussing?

It was in some form an image in the organic psyche of Copernicus. It was implicitly there. Bronowski sees it visually and relates it to the drawing by William Blake called "Glad Day," a drawing of a man astride the universe, high up in the heavens, standing, arms outstretched,

[6] Bronowski, *op. cit.*, pp. 21, 22.

next to the sun. It may be that Copernicus did indeed see such an image, or some equivalent of it, in a dream, or in a waking fantasy, and that this led him to his revolutionary conception of the cosmos, placing the sun at the center of things. But the question of whether Copernicus was actually aware of such an image would be irrelevant. It was there in principle in his psyche.

How shall we understand this? Bronowski writes, "His first step was a leap of imagination." Imagination is image-making. But image-making is not a conscious process. It cannot be deliberately done. We cannot create our images. The very reverse is true. Thus it would be that in the depths of the organic psyche, without his consciously willing it, an image of man close to the sun came to Copernicus and brought the sun to the center of his psychic universe. Then an image was present, not as a conscious belief, but as an operating fact within him. *It* saw the relationships of the universe in a new way in accordance with *its* center of reference. *It* restructured the facts and observations of astronomy. It was the vision that gave form to the work, that provided the basis for the discovery. It was a leap of image-making that carried Copernicus beyond the common-sense way of seeing the old facts. It carried him while he did the details of computation.

We may see the point underlying this in another example that Bronowski discusses. The ancient Greeks had a conception of matter in terms of atoms that is very different from the atomic theory of modern times; and yet the two conceptions stand in a close relation to each other. When, Bronowski writes, "John Dalton in 1808 first saw the structure of matter as we do today . . . what he took from the ancients was not their theory but something richer, their *image:* the atom." [7] That is to say, the link between the ancient and modern conceptions of the atom is not an intellectual link. It is not based upon the same calculations, or even upon the same kinds of observations of nature. But the connection lies in the *inner form of the conception,* which presented the pattern into which the data of atomic theory could be fitted.

The conception of the atom did not come to Dalton as an observation or as an inference drawn from the study of external materials. It came to him rather from within his own psyche. He used it consciously once it became strong enough in him so that he could see its significance. But its source was not in his consciousness. It came to him as an image that simply presented itself, as such things do. It was not sought; it came. It was not a creation of consciousness, but it was a creative factor itself that was brought forth out of the depths of the organic psyche.

We have spoken of the two kinds of protoplasmic imagery that arise out of the organic nature of the human species: the dynatypes and the cognitypes. The dynatypes are the images that provide the inner momentum and direction for individual activities and growth. The cognitypes are the core images that give form to human knowledge. They are two distinct aspects of the single creative process that is the essence of the human psyche. Since we have already discussed them in their distinctness, we now want to see how they work together in the unity of an un-

[7] *Ibid.,* p. 23. My italics.

folding personality. And for this goal the psychology of the creative scientist is a most instructive study.

One of the clearest examples of a cognitype is the atom. It is an image that recurs throughout history, and appears apparently spontaneously, in the most divergent cultures. Its forms vary; it may be called an atom or it may be called a monad; it may be related to matter, to the soul, or to the cosmos at large, the microcosm, or the macrocosm; but underlying its variations there is a common quality that seems to derive not from outer experience but from a pattern of cognition present as a potentiality in the structure of the psyche.

The cognitype of the atom is present as a possibility in the organic psyche of man. Thus it may leave its imprint upon the vision of reality expressed in an American Indian myth, in a pre-Socratic philosopher, in a medieval mathematician, and in a modern scientist groping toward discovery. The cognitype of the atom is present in all of them as a mold, an inner principle of formation and meaning that structures their experience of the world so that it can become knowledge.

But now the question is: into what form shall their image of the atom be placed? And, what is most important, of all the varieties of outer experience in which they participate, which will be more fruitfully understood when they are placed in the mold of the cognitype of the atom?

This is a question we can ask with respect to John Dalton. And we can give a provisional answer in terms of his work.

THE RESOURCES OF CREATIVE SCIENCE

The scientist groping toward discovery has access to two different kinds of resources. One is the mass of learned information and procedures of research that are part of his training and of his research in his field. The other resource is himself; or, to put it less personally, the other resource is his psyche in all its dimensions of depth containing the patterns of knowledge that can give form and meaning to his observations.

When the researcher has studied his evidence, observed and evaluated it, he has done all that his outward orientation makes possible. He then has to turn in another direction to find the meaning of his observations; and especially must he turn inward if he is dealing with material that calls for a new insight and a new form through which to reveal its significance. The research scientist is then called upon to do some research in an unexpected place, within himself, for it is there that the necessary new forms of understanding, the relevant cognitypes, will be found.

When we speak of it in these terms, saying that in order to make his discoveries the research scientist must turn into himself, it may seem that we are recommending that the scientist become subjective. Not at all. Nor are we saying what might even be more to the point, that the scientist achieves his new insight into truth on an objective level by taking a subjective step into himself.

Something of this is involved, but it should not be thought of in terms of subjectivity.

As we have already remarked, one of the most striking slogans of the scientists as they solidified their position in the nineteenth century was their stress on the impersonality of their researches. Their work was pictured as a severe dedication to objectivity, and it was thus that the scientist came to be thought of as a man without a personality.

This is, of course, a totally false view. It is false on the superficial level where the public image of the scientist is that of an absent-minded calculating machine. One has only to think of the warmth and social concern of such an apparently abstracted person as Albert Einstein to recognize that the scientist is indeed a human being. But the public image of the scientist as a man without a personality is false on a level much more fundamental than that, and in a way that is often not appreciated even by the scientists themselves. The scientist is a human being not only in his warmth, personal concerns, and sympathies, but much more importantly in the fact that he does indeed have an active and creative psyche, try as he may to give the impression that he is not using it.

It is true that the scientist is seldom a "personality" in the extraverted sense of the word; and also, at the other end of the spectrum, that he tends to be extremely skeptical and unwilling to concede that he has an "inner life" at all. The traditional attitudes of the natural sciences have directed him toward much more tangible areas of experience and observation. But he does possess, like all other human beings, a personality in depth, a psyche that is dynamically involved in all his activities. He may not value it consciously, but it plays a highly important role in his work nonetheless. It provides the resources for his personal development, his dedication to his work, his insights, hunches, and conceptual ways of knowing. And all these are derived from a level of his psyche, his organic psyche, that is much more fundamental than the essentially personal, more or less subjective aspects of his personality.

There is an interesting and valuable distinction to be made in this connection with respect to the personal and impersonal levels of the psyche. At one level may be found the subjectivities of the individual's life, his personal attitudes and predilections, intimate wishes and fears, hopes and repressions. But this is a stratum of the psyche that is relatively close to the surface of consciousness. It is not in touch with the nonpersonal resources of the organic psyche. It is the area of the psyche that contains what we spoke of earlier as the *familial images* and the *environmental self*. What Alfred Adler spoke of as the individual's *style of life* and his *guiding fiction* are also to be found on this level of the psyche to which C. G. Jung referred in general as the *personal unconscious*. Terminology in this regard varies in the several approaches to depth psychology; but it is an essential conception that is involved here, and it is found in the thinking of Sigmund Freud and Otto Rank as well.

Keeping in mind the subjective side of the psyche, we can appreciate the authentic reasons for which the scientist has tended to shy away from the suggestion that he approach his scientific problems in terms of psychology. He has thought of psychology in terms of the usual clichés of psychoanalysis, and he has thus assumed that for him to approach his scientific work psychologically would involve him in the subjective side of his life. He has correctly judged that this would be quite irrelevant for his scientific investigations, but he has not realized that quite another psychologic way is possible.

Balancing the subjective side of the personality is another aspect of the organic psyche. This is essentially impersonal and nonsubjective. In it the more-than-personal, the formative and cognitive principles of man's life are expressed. These principles are the dynatypes and the cognitypes of which we have spoken. The scientist can turn to this part of himself in a spirit of impersonality and objective search that is fully in accord with his scientific dedication.

We have said that when the research scientist reaches an impasse in his attempts at discovery it is time for him to do some research into himself. Perhaps in saying this it sounds as though we are repeating the standard psychoanalytic advice that is given to the writer who can go no further in his novel, or to the artist whose painting has run out of inspiration. He is advised to turn the spotlight inward to find the blockage within his personality. But here we are recommending for the scientist as well as for all creative types of persons an approach that is operationally the very opposite of the psychoanalytic way. And the difference has important consequences.

We are not recommending at all that in the midst of his work the scientist turn away from his studies to dissect his personal life in the self-conscious style of the analytic psychologists. If he did that, he would be following the one psychologic procedure that surely short-circuits the creative process; for it is the diagnostic, self-analytical habit of mind of the "psychological era" that has kept the modern personality walking a treadmill for the past two generations. Having been conceived and oriented in terms of psychopathology, this analytic style has inevitably stymied the creative process of personal growth. A long stride beyond it is therefore overdue.[8]

The *holistic depth psychology* which we have been describing is an attempt to take this step and build a knowledge of man that will do justice to his capacities. Our goal in doing this is more than intellectual. Our time in history urgently requires an understanding of the workings of the human personality that will enable modern man to draw forth and fulfill more of his potentialities. And these potentialities involve something much more than man's capacity for infinite self-gratification, pleasure-seeking, and subjective happiness; they involve the progressive extension of knowledge together with impersonal service in the enhancement of life.

Having come this far in the development of science,

[8] See Ira Progoff, *The Death and Rebirth of Psychology,* Chapters VII and VIII.

modern man is not free to stop. As much knowledge as he has is a dangerous thing, especially because it is accompanied by so little understanding of man himself while it has made the most powerful tools and weapons accessible to every man. It has therefore become more important than ever that we move onward in our knowledge and extend the frontiers of science further still. It is essential, even if only to protect us from what science has already done. And yet we have also to face the fact that the difficulties impeding really major breakthroughs in discovery, the establishment of new vantage points and orientations, are much greater now than they were in the early days of science. Habits and styles of thinking, the protocols of proper scientific procedure, now fence in the freedom that was felt by the early scientific pioneers. And today the discovery of radically new formulations is impeded, perhaps paradoxically, by the very mass and complexity of the knowledge that has already been accumulated.

It has thus come to be of the most fundamental importance to modern man that he gain access to a psychological conception that can prove itself on the testing ground of creative achievements, particularly in the field of science. The scientific researcher has become the prototype of the creative individual in modern times, for he is working on the frontier where the new relationship between man and reality is being formed. Unfortunately, he is seldom able to feel psychologically prepared for the role that is being thrust upon him. The nature of his previous discipline has precluded any sustained contact with the resources within himself, with the depths of his organic psyche. He has therefore not had occasion in the past to familiarize himself with the creative workings of the inner life of man, nor has he gained access to it to discover how it can be of use to him. And yet the scientific researcher needs this knowledge very profoundly now, as profoundly as he himself is needed by modern civilization.

To meet this need, we require an understanding of man that can be translated into practical procedures for increasing the productivity of imaginative insight in scientific research and in such other fields as business enterprise, and the arts. Holistic depth psychology is moving into a position where it may well be able to fill this need. It holds great promise especially because it does not falsify the creative process in man by describing personality in terms of pathology. It remembers that the keynote of creativity is potentiality.[9] The knowledge that depth psychology seeks to develop is a knowledge of how the seeds of latent capacity in man grow to fulfillment, and of how the processes involved in this can become more fruitful.

THE SCIENTIST AS A PERSON IN GROWTH

In this perspective we can discuss anew our recommendation that when the scientific researcher or the creative

[9] See the related conception of Gardner Murphy in his recent book, *Human Potentialities,* New York, Basic Books, 1958.

person in general has reached an impasse in his work, it is time for him to do some research into himself. This means turning his attention inward, and to take such a step is often exceedingly difficult for the person who has been accustomed to directing his energies entirely outward. The inner world often seems unreal to such a person, especially in his first contacts with it; but he soon is able to realize that it is real indeed, especially when he perceives that it is, and always has been, the instigator and secret director of his outer activities.

The most important and indeed crucial point here is the realization that the psyche is not by any means identical with mental contents of a subjective kind. The fullness of the psyche reaches far beyond the personal memories, fears, and repressions with which it has usually been identified. These comprise only a relatively small portion of the psyche as a whole. They constitute actually that part of the "unconscious" that relates specifically to individuality; and they do not include that much larger and more fundamental part of the organic psyche that belongs to the generality of mankind, the tendencies and patterns of human nature that underlie the beliefs and behavior of the individual person.

These basic principles and images of the organic psyche are not personal and subjective. There is an element of uniqueness about them because they vary from person to person in the individual forms in which they are expressed. But this apparent uniqueness may be quite misleading.

What is important in these images is not their differences, which are experienced as subjectivities. What is important, rather, is their underlying sameness as formative factors that give shape and direction to the personality. They have an objective quality, much as the principles governing the circulation of the blood are generic to man and are objective in their form, even though the rate of circulation and the type of blood may vary from individual to individual.

These principles and images of the organic psyche, the dynatypes and cognitypes of which we have spoken, are the objective and generic components upon which individual personalities and individual conceptions of reality are based. They are more than personal, and their essential quality is the very opposite of subjectivity. It is these objective and dynamic factors in himself that the scientist would meet if he would turn to do research within himself when his creative work had reached an impasse.

Would this mean that the scientist would then turn from analyzing the subject matter of his specialty in science to analyzing the depth contents of his organic psyche? No, because the analytic attitude in psychologic practice has shown itself to be a highly inefficient means of achieving personality growth. The psyche is not built piece by piece as a machine is built. It grows organically out of its seed as living matter grows in nature.

As a rosebush grows, a human being grows. The flower that is potential in the seed of the rosebush is not visible there; so also the capacities of the human being do not disclose themselves before the appropriate moment of maturity, before this particular human being is ready.

Though one may wish to see the rose beforehand, to get some intimation of how it will look when it finally does appear, there is no way of seeing it ahead of time. One cannot analyze the components that will produce the rose. Truly they are not there yet, and will not be present until the moment when the rose actually emerges from the bud.

The creative process in nature is one of unfoldment. The seed contains a possibility, a possibility whose nature is defined in advance, but whose reality awaits a process of unfoldment that cannot be varied from the pattern of growth built into the protoplasmic seed of the species. Man grows in accordance with a similar principle of nature. Certain possibilities are present in the seed of his being. Some disclose themselves physically as the body matures. Others are psychologic and make their presence felt as goals and directions of behavior and as the patterns of thought and belief. These are the guiding and emergent principles of the organic psyche, the dynatypes and the cognitypes. The life growth of the individual human being, as he goes about his innate protoplasmic task of becoming a person, is the outer unfoldment of these generic and objective seed-images.

The life of the scientist is the unfoldment of such an image. It is his dynatype, the image that propels him forward from within, directing him toward goals he can see only dimly and distantly but to which he is dedicated with all his being. It is this protoplasmic seed-image, this dynatype unfolding within him that gives the creative scientist, in Bronowski's words, "his sense of pleasure and of adventure and that excitement which keeps him working late into the night when all the useful typists have gone home at five o'clock. *He is personally involved in his work,* as the poet is in his, and as the artist is in the painting." [10]

He is personally involved in his work because his work is the embodiment of the unfolding image that is progressively giving meaning to his life. It is his *opus,* his art work, and as such it embodies his life. He lives it, and it lives him. It is his existence concretely expressed. Thus, as he carries through his opus, the scientist participates in the ongoing, encompassing unity of life. His work is a concrete bit of immortality in which he shares, whether he ever places his personal signature to an enduring discovery or not.

The work itself, carrying the unfoldment of his basic life image, is for him a direct link to life which he experiences spontaneously as meaningful in the fullness of his being beyond all conscious or rational questionings. This is the form of meaningful life for him; and with it, the stamp of his unique existence is placed upon something that is much more than personal. The opus in which he expresses his life dynatype carries him beyond his individuality. It enlarges him by relating him objectively to the continuity of life. And with this the scientist experiences a qualitative sense of immortality *via his scientific art work.* Through it, he participates in life meaningfully beyond the confines of his mortal existence; and with it, therefore, he satisfies the requirements of the

[10] Bronowski, *op. cit.,* p. 16, my italics.

survival drive that is deep in his protoplasmic nature. He is connected to life ongoingly and transpersonally by means of the dynatypal seed-image that unfolds within him while he carries on his opus outside.

Now the question arises of how we can describe the dynatype that places its imprint upon the life of the scientist. Shall we give it a specific name? Shall we say that it is the seed-image of the "seeker for truth"? Or shall we call it the image of the "tinkerer" or of the idly curious, the skeptic, or the seeker for unity in life? Many such descriptions would be applicable to the scientist, for there are many aspects to his nature. But perhaps at its best the dynatype of the scientist may be described as the protoplasmic image of the one who seeks truth in the natural world and seeks it through unitary principles. "All science," Bronowski writes, "is the search for unity in hidden likenesses." [11]

It would seem, however, that the particular designation we use for the dynatype of the scientist is not important. What is truly important is the recognition that a dynatypal image is indeed at work there. Scientific discovery, despite its appearance of outward objectivity, is not the work of an automaton, but of a human being engaged in growing; and the growth that takes place is the unfoldment of a potentiality present in the seed of the scientist as a person. This potentiality is expressed as an image, or perhaps more clearly as a *type,* a tendency of growth imprinted on the original seed-nature of the individual organism.

11 *Ibid.,* p. 23.

However we may define and describe the specific nature of these *types,* which contain the implicit patterns of growth in persons, their essential quality is an active propulsiveness that draws forward the underlying process of personality development. These *types* have a dynamic quality which embodies the creative operation of the organic psyche. As the *dynatypes* unfold, therefore, the psyche as a whole fulfills itself and grows toward maturity.

The process is a unitary one in which is included the unfolding image, the goal of the activity, the primary instinctual energy necessary to carry it forward, and the unconscious understanding of how to bring the work to completion. All this is present in principle at the depth of the psyche and is drawn outward into life as the dynatype unfolds in a concrete *opus.* Much of the knowledge needed for the work is drawn from this source within the psyche itself. In man the supply of knowledge is not as direct as the native architectural sense demonstrated by the hummingbird in building her nest, but it does involve psychic levels that are far more fundamental than learned behavior.

The process by which the dynatype matures stirs the entire psyche into activity, especially the dark, subliminal levels of cognition. Thus, when the person is totally and spontaneously engaged in the process of dynatypal growth, many perceptions and insights come to him directly with a strength and acuity beyond his ordinary capacity. The unconscious psyche then becomes much more sensitive to the world around it, especially to those facts of life that pertain to its emerging dynatype.

Often, also, the activity of the dynatype arouses deeper and more fundamental cognitypes, especially when the image that is being enacted involves a search for truth, as in the case of the scientist or the philosopher. Thus we find that in the intensity of the search for truth that is essential for the opus of the creative scientist, profound images may appear out of the depths of the psyche spontaneously—i.e., unsought by the conscious ego—providing a conception or context of thought that raises a problem to a new level of insight.

This has occurred many times in the history of science, with respect to the theory of energy, gravity, the atom, and molecular structure among other discoveries. The images aroused in this connection are the cognitypes. They are brought to the level of conscious awareness of the deep psyche in activity, in search, and in its inward struggling. They may appear quite suddenly in waking moments of intensity; or they may come silently and surreptitiously, but no less effectively, in dreams.

We see here a very important principle of depth psychology at work. The fundamental and the most constructive quality of what we speak of as *depth* is *growth in action.* Latent capacities of the organic psyche are coming forth, are unfolding, are developing. This is depth showing its face in the world.

But what is taking place while this is happening? The organic psyche is being stirred into a ferment that reaches into the length and breadth of its being when the dynatype is engaged in fulfilling its potentialities. The dynatype is *in growth,* and growth has an activating effect upon the wholeness of the organism. This does indeed lead to inner tensions, but these are tensions that are creative in essence and in outcome. Especially so, since the turmoil within the person stirs deeper and more fundamental cognitypes than have been effective in consciousness before. Then additional insights and awareness, greater even than what had been originally sought by the dynatype, become available for creative use. Our understanding of this process opens great practical possibilities, and is therefore worth investigating more closely.

9 * Psychological tools for creative work

KEKULÉ THE CHEMIST AND THE SYMBOL OF THE SERPENT

A very interesting and instructive example of how creative psychic events take place in scientific work is the discovery of the structural theory of organic chemistry. In 1858, August Kekulé published his discovery of the tetravalence and self-linking of carbon; and some years later he made further discoveries concerning the benzene structure.

These discoveries were of the greatest importance for the development of organic chemistry, both theoretically and in industry. In 1890, on the twenty-fifth anniversary of his benzene theory, Kekulé was honored at a festival at the Berlin City Hall. There he gave a speech in which he described some of the intimate experiences that led him to his discoveries; and these are of very great significance for our understanding of the depth processes that operate in the psyche of the creative scientist. The speech was recently translated and published in the *Journal of Chemical Education*,[1] from which I quote, following the comments of the editors with regard to the background of the text.

In his talk, Kekulé first makes a remark that reflects his personal experience about the way new knowledge is reached. "It is said that a genius recognizes truth without knowing the evidence for it. I do not doubt," Kekulé states, "that even in ancient times this kind of thinking occurred. Would Pythagoras have offered up a hecatomb if he had recognized his famous theorem only after finding a way to prove it?"

New insights do not depend on the outward observations, measurements, and analyses of the subject matter. The crucial step in gaining the new knowledge comes from within, and its validity may be perceived, or at least *felt*, before it can be outwardly proved. That was the way it was with Kekulé himself. The crucial step in opening his understanding came from within, and it came in a symbolic form from the relevant imagery of the organic psyche. There remained the task of relating his inner

[1] *Journal of Chemical Education*, "August Kekulé and the Birth of the Structural Theory of Organic Chemistry in 1858," O. Theodor Benfey (translator), pp. 21-23. I am very grateful to Dr. Arthur H. Fischer for calling my attention to this speech.

vision to his outward researches. But that could be accomplished without too great difficulty, since at that stage of the work it is a matter of professional competence and not of inspiration. This task of relating the outer and the inner to each other is of central importance in the creative work of the scientist, as we shall presently see. And we should take note as well at this point that this is the task of the creative artist in every field, for the *opus*, the art work, represents the inner vision molded into a material embodiment. The task of carrying this out with honesty and meaningfulness is the *work* that is the central challenge before the artist and the testing ground of his growth as a creative person.

How did Kekulé receive the insights that made his major discoveries possible? He tells first of how his "structural theory" was found.

Kekulé had been visiting in London and had taken a late bus ride across the city. On the bus, he tells us, "I fell into a reverie, and lo, the atoms were gamboling before my eyes! Whenever hitherto, these diminutive beings had appeared to me, they had always been in motion; but up to that time I had never been able to discern the nature of their motion. Now, however, I saw how, frequently, two smaller atoms united to form a pair; how a larger one embraced the two smaller ones; how still larger ones kept hold of three or even four of the smaller; whilst the whole kept whirling in a giddy dance. I saw how the larger ones formed a chain, dragging the smaller ones after them but only at the ends of the chain. I saw what our past master, Kopp, my highly honored teacher and friend, has depicted with such charm in his *Molekular-Welt;* but I saw it long before him. The cry of the conductor, 'Clapham Road,' awakened me from my dreaming; but I spent a part of the night in putting on paper at least sketches of these dream forms. This was the origin of the 'Structural Theory.' "

When we consider Kekulé's way of working toward scientific discovery, we realize that he was a person who possessed a spontaneous appreciation of the "image-making faculty" of the psyche. He was apparently in the habit of making use of this faculty in his chemical researches. Thus he tells us that in times past he had permitted himself to fall into a reverie in order to "see" the inner workings of the atom before his mind's eye. And there he had indeed been able to see it, but not in the detail that his scientific knowledge required. He had, he tells us, been able to see the atoms "in motion"; but he needed to delve into "the nature of their motion," and for this it seems it was necessary for him to move deeper into the subliminal levels of his psyche than he had done in previous reveries.

It seems that the reverie into which Kekulé lapsed while taking the late bus to Clapham Road took him to greater psychic depths than his previous excursions. There are many possible reasons for this about which we can offer some hypotheses a little later on. Here, however, we must merely call attention to the spontaneous realization by a research scientist that the deliberate use of fantasy constitutes an important source of new empirical knowledge.

In his talk at the meeting honoring him, Kekulé went on to tell how he happened to make his second great discovery, the benzene theory. "During my stay in Ghent," he said, "I resided in elegant bachelor quarters on the main thoroughfare. My study, however, faced a narrow side-alley and no daylight penetrated it. For the chemist who spends his day in the laboratory this mattered little. I was sitting writing at my textbook, but the work did not progress; my thoughts were elsewhere. I turned my chair to the fire and dozed. Again the atoms were gamboling before my eyes. This time the smaller groups kept modestly in the background. My mental eye, rendered more acute by repeated visions of this kind, could now distinguish larger structures of manifold conformation; long rows, sometimes more closely fitted together all twining and twisting in snake-like motion. But look! What was that? One of the snakes had seized hold of its own tail and the form whirled mockingly before my eyes. As if by a flash of lightning I awoke; and this time also I spent the rest of the night in working out the consequences of the hypothesis."

And Kekulé concluded with a wonderful flourish, "Let us learn to dream, gentlemen, then perhaps we shall learn the truth."

Now what can we learn from the advice of this great pioneer in modern chemistry?

The first lesson is that we pay serious and respectful attention to the seemingly pointless fantasies of the psyche. What, indeed, does a snake have to do with the structure of the atom? In point of fact, the snake biting its tail and so forming a circle that rolls without end is a primordial symbol that appears in the most diverse forms in the mythologies of many cultures. Under the name of "Ourobouros" it has been recognized as a widely recurring pattern in the imagery of the organic psyche, and interpreting it has provided a most exciting exercise for scholars of mythological symbolism.[2]

There is no question that any rational person would have a right to ask: What does benzene have to do with the *Ourobouros?* And yet the testimony of Kekulé indicates that the appearance of the image of the Ourobouros in his fantasies was closely related to his discovery of the benzene ring. To understand specifically what took place in the psyche of Kekulé, we must give the entire matter closer consideration; but we are forced by this very fact to recognize that the seemingly irrational symbolism of the psychic depths contains, strange as it may seem, a striking relevance for the disciplined intellect. It is all the more important, therefore, that the scientist be able to comprehend what this relevance is, in order that he may make use of it.

The second lesson we may learn from Kekulé is then the importance not only of becoming aware of the organic psyche but of developing the capacity to perceive its imagery in meaningful ways. Kekulé's remark that his "mental eye" had been "rendered more acute by repeated visions of this kind" is indicative of the diligence with which he searched his unconscious psyche for in-

[2] See particularly Erich Neumann, *The Origins and History of Consciousness.* New York, Pantheon, 1954.

sights. And yet in that era before depth psychology Kekulé could have been acting upon little more than intuitive recognition of the creative resources of human personality. We can only wonder and surmise to what heights scientific research can reach when scientists make a conscious attempt to draw the imagery of the organic psyche into the service of their studies. This is surely one of the major contributions that the new holistic depth psychology will make in the coming generation.

Let us now look closer to see what is involved in a process such as Kekulé describes. In him, the dynatype of the scientist, the seeker for truth in the natural world, was strongly expressed. He was enacting it as an image securely rooted at the organic level of his psyche.

Consequently his activities displayed the main characteristics of the dynatypes in operation. They brought forth large quantities of psychic energy; and this gave a quality of intensity and fervor to the psyche. Also, in his activities, these energies were channelized in a manner and in a direction that would fulfill the goal implicit in the dynatype. And this goal was embodied in specific works of consciousness, the many small and special tasks that comprise the everyday life of the scientist.

Thus, in our framework for thinking about the creative unfoldment of the person, Kekulé was living out an image that derived from the depth of his psyche; and this image supplied the energy, the direction, and the dedication of his life. The dynatype of the seeker for truth in the realm of nature was the image working in the background of his activities. It provided their goal and their meaning.

Through the dynatype unfolding in him, Kekulé could feel himself to be participating in what we have spoken of as a *survival form,* a symbolic connection with the on-going unity of life.

The world view of science with its aspirations and criteria for knowledge was the survival form that was effective for Kekulé, for it provided the framework of personal meaning for his scientific activities. In this sense, Kekulé's persistent search for new understanding embodied in his personality the protoplasmic striving for life that is inherent in man.

This protoplasmic striving is what we have spoken of as the *survival drive* that is fundamental in all species, but in man is expressed culturally as well as biologically and so becomes a drive toward *qualitative survival.* As we have seen, the biological urge toward self-preservation transforms itself in man and becomes a striving for an experience of unity with life that is essentially an extension of life in symbolic terms.

Immortality, which means the unending survival of the individual, is experienced then as a real fact, but not in so fixed or literal a form. It is experienced rather as a qualitative immortality. It brings an inner, often unarticulated conviction of participating in the future, far beyond one's mortal span of years; but this survival is in terms of values that are felt to have a higher or ultimate truth. Thus, as Kekulé enacted his dynatype of the scientist, he was in that very act fulfilling his survival drive by participating in an aspect of life that had the greatest reality and meaning for him.

DEPTH DYNAMICS OF DISCOVERY

From the holistic point of view, as we have earlier indicated, this has the largest implications. The survival drive, which is rooted in the protoplasmic core of personality, expresses itself most fully in those processes that carry forward the creative growth of the individual. We often find, therefore, a virtual identity between the dynatype unfolding in the person and the survival drive.

Often the work that represents the goal or is the achievement of the dynatype, the opus or art work, is the concrete embodiment of the person's relation to life. It is the objective entity that carries the possibility of his individual survival, and it therefore stands forth as a marker of the enduring significance of the individual's transitory existence. In line with this, we find that the vast amount of energy in the organism which the evolutionary process reserves for the crises of self-preservation, and which is always available to the survival drive in man, is eventually expressed via the dynatypal images. This is one explanation of the fact that the process of creative growth in man often seems to have illimitable resources of energy at its disposal. Creative growth and survival have indeed much in common.

When the creative images are emerging constructively, large sums of energy, psychologically and physiologically, are directed into the individual's activities. But what happens when the growth process is blocked? What happens when an impasse arises, specifically in the case of the scientist whose vast dynatypal energies have been expressed in his work in a rich conscious development, and who suddenly finds a roadblock before him so that he cannot proceed? For whatever reason, whether it be shortage of materials or a shortage of ideas, if the creative opus bogs down, what is the next step?

We may approach this question in terms of Kekulé's experience, for it seems to fit the situation he described in his speech. His thinking had come to an impasse, the supply of insights into his problem seemed to have dwindled away, leaving him no alternative but to stop the conscious processes of research. To continue them would only have resulted in an anxious pressing and a tension that would have put still a further strain upon the creative processes. He found himself then in a situation of *frustration,* a frustration that is almost unavoidable in creative work whether in science or any other field.

When the creative work is proceeding well, the dynatypal energies of which we have been speaking move abundantly out into the tasks at hand. But when the inevitable stoppages appear, the avenues of energy expression close. Energy cannot then move outward into life. It dams up, but its inherently dynamic nature forces it to continue in motion, no matter in which direction it moves. It moves away then from the level of conscious awareness, since it finds no channel there. It moves toward the nonconscious depths of the psyche, and in doing so it withdraws attention from the immediate concerns of life. Imperceptibly and without realizing what is happening, the person slides off into reverie, or into the floating spaces of fantasy.

What is taking place then? When reverie or fantasying occurs, it is a sign that the dynatypal energy has altered its course and is moving backward and downward into the psyche where it prods dormant contents of the unconscious into activity.

This "descent" of energy into the psyche moves by stages that can be marked off in a general way, corresponding to the levels of depth in the structure of personality. As the energy descends to the reverie level, which is not far at all from the surface level of consciousness, it awakens wishful thoughts, old desires, or passions prohibited by society; and it stirs them up for a new flurry of excitement. If the situation continues, the energy will move still deeper into the psyche. It will then awaken old memories. These may be memories of experiences that have been forgotten because of passing time and dwindling interest; or they may be memories that have been repressed because their painfulness could not be borne by the conscious mind.

When the impasse in the creative work activates the film of wishfulness that is on the surface of the unconscious, the result is much fantasying, subjectively and symbolically done. This has its uses at certain times, but essentially it is an idle activity of the psyche. It is an expenditure of energy in terms of personal vanity, and its ego-centeredness diverts the person ever further from the selflessness that creativity requires. It does serve a constructive function, however, and this is mainly as a safety valve that permits a release from the tension of continuous concentration. The very subjectivity of wishful reverie is its value on occasion, especially when it balances the overrigorous objectivity that some disciplines demand.

If the dynatypal energy descends further into the psyche it arouses the memories, both pleasant and traumatic, that were slumbering there. Here it may be that something troublesome will be awakened, old angers and anxieties that forcibly distract the person from his creative tasks. These are the dangerous demons of the psyche which, like sleeping animals, had best be left untouched. If they are aroused in the course of the frustrations of creative work, one may expect disturbances of greater or less seriousness, depending upon the individual. These are among the hazards, the calculated risks, of all creative undertakings.

These two classes of psychic contents, the wishes and the memories, both belong to a relatively superficial and essentially subjective level of what has been called the unconscious. This is the area of the psyche that Freud described under the phrase, the *"Unconscious Repressed,"* and it is what Jung, in a somewhat different form of reference, spoke of as the *"Personal Unconscious."*

Now let us suppose that the energy continues to descend into the depths of the psyche. We must note in passing that the greater the strength of the dynatype that is involved as the active image in the individual, the greater will be the force with which it penetrates into the

deeper levels of the psyche when it is frustrated in its
work. This has to do in the first place with the nature
of the image itself, especially with whether it is an image
that carries a great intensity of energy as does the dynatype of the Seeker for Truth.

It depends also upon how securely and how deeply the
image is placed in the structure of the individual psyche.
If the dynatype is strong and is profoundly placed in the
psyche, it will express itself with a very large amount of
energy, the energy of the survival drive, whether the
direction of that energy is outward in the world or inward into the depths of the psyche.

When in this sort of situation the creative person is
frustrated in his work so that the energy of the dynatype
turns inward, it moves with great force in its effort to
fulfill itself. Without the individual's realizing what is
happening, since it is an event that takes place far from
consciousness, the dynatypal energy plunges into the organic depths of the psyche. There it activates the protoplasmic imagery that is latent in the psyche, those images
that are generic to the species and, in principle, are universal in man.

These fundamental images, which are at the protoplasmic depths of the organic psyche, contain the core of
the symbolic experiences with which in varying forms
man has related himself to the universe in every period
of history. These are the images that contain the pristine
intimations of meaning in man's life. They are deep in
the organic psyche at its protoplasmic level, and while
men subscribe consciously to the institutionalized form in

which they appear in history, the essence of these images is in their primary form at the organic depths of the psyche.

Here their inner principle is contained latently as a potentiality of experience and as a pattern of awareness that brings insight into reality transcending the ordinary bounds of human perception. These transcendent insights, which come out of the protoplasmic core of the psyche, carry a sense of ultimate knowledge and conviction, and thus they are experienced as *metaphysically* true. When, therefore, a person is brought into contact with these images within himself he finds that, regardless of the period of history in which he is living, he is brought under the sway of a search for meaning that is essentially a religious quest.

This is the fate of the artists and poets, the philosophers and mystics in every age and culture who discover, when the protoplasmic imagery of the psyche is awakened in them, that they have been brought, without their wishing it, into a realm of *ultimate concerns*. They have been brought into an encounter with meaning that involves the ultimate significance of man's life in the cosmos. This encounter comes about essentially as a by-product of their creative undertakings, and especially as a result of the frustrations they have met in their work. Once it has happened, however, it immeasurably enlarges the scope of their work, bringing to it a dimension of depth and spiritual perspective that multiplies the meaningfulness of whatever specific endeavor the individual is following.

We are increasingly observing this to be true of creative scientists. In the frustrations of their work, the intensity of the creative image working in them inevitably forces energy inward and downward into the depths of the organic psyche. Here the scientist becomes involved in something much more fundamental than the outer materials of his research. He encounters the ultimate questions of life, receives some symbolic intimations of what their meaning may be, and is challenged in the wholeness of his being to relate these intimations to the kind of reality in which he feels most at home, the realities of the physical world.

This last step is inherent in the dynatype of the scientist, for his is the image of the seeker for *truth in nature*. He is thus stimulated to seek the proximate truths of nature, and also something more. The scientist who is brought into touch with the depths of the psyche finds himself drawn into the service of two masters simultaneously. One is the need for knowledge of the physical world; the other is the intuitive awareness of a larger meaning beyond this knowledge. He requires them both, and therefore the secret theme in the life of many a creative scientist is his attempt to draw together, at least to his personal inner satisfaction, his knowledge of physical reality and his symbolic intimations of ultimate reality. This has been true of many generations from Copernicus to Einstein; and it may be especially true in the generations to come.

We shall have occasion to return to this question, for it is a matter of great significance to modern man. First, however, let us continue our task of tracing the descent of energy into the psyche when its expression is frustrated by some condition in the outer world.

It activates first the subjective levels of the psyche, the realm of wishes and of memories. As it continues inward it reaches the nonpersonal, generic patterns of imagery that are inherent in the human species. This is the depth from which the dynatypes emerge, and also the cognitypes of which we have spoken. But most important, it is on this level that the organic symbolism of the psyche reaches beyond itself and gives man his intimation of realities that transcend and irradiate his existence.

For the question of how new discoveries are drawn by the scientist out of the depth of the psyche, the cognitypes have major significance. The cognitypes are the patterns of imagery that provide the forms of human knowledge. As the scientific investigator reaches an impasse in his work so that, in frustration, his energy moves away from his work and inward into the psyche, a new source of insight is brought into play. Now the images of the deep psyche become available as *models* for the interpretation of nature. Thus it was that in Kekulé's reverie the ancient symbol of the Ourobouros, the snake that bites its own tail forming a self-contained circle, came forth spontaneously. It emerged from the depth levels of the organic psyche in Kekulé, and provided him unexpectedly with the *model* for his benzene theory.

Perhaps, however, we should not say that the symbol of the circular snake came spontaneously to Kekulé. It came to him without any deliberate act of preparation; it was totally unguided, and in this sense it was indeed spontaneous. It "just happened" to him when he fell into his state of reverie. But such a spontaneous event and insight became possible only after much else had taken place psychologically.

For this to happen it was necessary first that Kekulé be engaged consciously in a work of creativity, a work of dedication based upon an image possessing great strength deep in his psyche. This image was the dynatype of the scientist, the seeker for truth in nature, which Kekulé was enacting and which he had already fulfilled in large degree through the self-discipline demanded by his studies.

The crucial event in the process, however, was the frustration that Kekulé felt in his scientific work. His research had reached an impasse, at least temporarily, and he did not have an answer ready at hand. But then, reacting to the situation of frustration, the dynatypal energy attached to the image of the seeker for truth turned inward and traversed the various levels of psychic depth which we have described. Ultimately it drew forth from the organic psyche a cognitype of ancient psychic vintage. And this image came to the fore in a reverie, a light dream which was sufficient in that case to bring the relevant depth symbolism of the psyche into the field of conscious awareness.

The fact of frustration in the work of scientific discovery seems to have played a central role in the eventual outcome. Psychoanalytic theory has traditionally spoken of frustration as a prelude to aggression on the part of the frustrated individual. "Frustration and aggression" has been a key phrase, even a sort of slogan, for psychologic thinking of several persuasions. And yet it would seem, to judge from the events that we have been describing, that frustration does not necessarily lead to aggression at all. Quite the contrary, it seems instead to lead to a deepening of the entire process of psychological growth so that it culminates eventually in a creative outcome. In fact, because of the crucial role that frustration plays in sending the energy inward to richer sources of inspiration in the depths of the psyche, we should speak not of "frustration and aggression" but of "frustration and creativity."

In all of this, one cannot say enough to emphasize the importance of Kekulé's attitude of openness toward the images that came to him from the depths of his psyche. He had learned to watch for them, to scrutinize them carefully with his mind's eye, and to treat them with respectful attention. He understood that the main resource for the scientist, as it is for the artist, lies in the depth of his own psychic being. And Kekulé realized as well that the most instructive messages from the deep psyche may come either in dreams or in a style of spontaneous, unguided image formation that is comparable to dreams but is more accessible to consciousness. It was the perception of this process of image-making that he seems to have encouraged in himself, demonstrating thereby an intuitive awareness of one of the basic processes of the psyche; and in this also he sought to develop a greater facility through practice. In this regard, too, Kekulé was not only a great innovator in the field of chemistry but he was a forerunner of practices by which modern depth psychology undertakes to expedite the creative processes of the psyche.

RELIGIOUS EXPERIENCE IN SCIENTIFIC WORK

In his work, seeking new forms of scientific understanding from the depths of the psyche, Kekulé could only wait and watch, hoping that the relevant image would come to him. When that image finally did appear, a further and most important step remained. It was necessary then that Kekulé recognize the significance of the image, irrelevant though it might seem when it appeared in the strange symbolic form of the circular snake. He had to perceive the relationship between the psychic symbol, the snake, and the chemical structure of benzene. He had to perceive the connection between the image and the empiric facts; and he had to work out the details that would bind them together in a meaningful way.

This is the most difficult step in the entire creative process, and it has the greatest impact upon the personality as a whole. It is the step of unification in which the empiric facts of external reality are interpreted in terms of cognitive images drawn from the inner world of the psyche. The inner and the outer are therefore merged by the scientist, who in this sense performs the very same role as the artist, giving form to unformed matter, giving meaning to previously meaningless facts.

A most instructive commentary upon this process was recently provided for us by the physicist, winner of the Nobel prize, Wolfgang Pauli (1900-1958). Pauli, who has himself made some major discoveries in the field of physics, undertook to study the psychologic processes at work in the discoveries of Johannes Kepler. His conclusions are all the more enlightening because they reflect not only the work of Kepler but the experiences of a modern scientist as well. [3]

Pauli marked off two essential phases in the process of scientific discovery. The first is the observation of nature, for always the facts of the outer world must be the basis and starting point of study. We begin, Pauli says, by "adjusting our knowledge to external objects." [4] But then a second step is necessary. Kepler first observed the raw facts of nature as far as he could perceive them by the light of the conceptions known in his day. But his task lay in finding the meaning of what he observed, and of placing that meaning within the framework of a view of the world. This meaning, being conceptual, was not to be found in the external world; and so Kepler turned inward, seeking and finding within himself the symbolic conceptions which provided the form for his new understanding of the raw, external facts.

In other words, Kepler turned his attention into the depths of his organic psyche in a way that was comparable

[3] See Pauli's monograph, "The Influence of Archetypal Ideas on the Scientific Theories of Kepler," which forms the second part of the book entitled, *The Interpretation of Nature and Psyche*, Bollingen Series LI, New York, Pantheon Books, 1955.
[4] *Ibid.*, p. 208.

to the process we observed in the discoveries of August Kekulé. He did not necessarily follow the same procedure of deliberate reverie, but the net psychologic effect was the same. It involved a direction of energy downward into the nonconscious levels of the psyche, there to activate and, in Pauli's phrase, to "bring to light the archetypal images used in the creation of our scientific concepts." And Pauli hastens to point out that both of these steps are essential parts of the integral works of discovery. "Only by combining both these directions of research," only by moving both outward toward the observable world of nature and inward toward the images that provide the forms and models of knowledge, "may complete understanding be obtained." [5]

What does Pauli's study of Kepler and his own experience as a creative scientist indicate about the qualities of these images? In the case of Kepler, one is struck by the symbolic conception of the cosmos "to which Kepler remained faithful from his early youth." It was a "view of the correspondence between the sun and its surrounding planets" and it included an "abstract spherical picture of the Trinity as primary." This was a symbolic view to which Kepler adhered in terms of emotional conviction. It was a conception of the cosmos in which he believed as a personal religious faith and with all the intensity of the deep psyche. It therefore held, as Pauli interprets it, the primary place in his psychologic life; and it provided the foundation for the studies that led to his discoveries in physics. "Because Kepler," Pauli says, "looks at the sun

5 *Ibid.,* pp. 208-209.

and the planets with this archetypal image in the background he believes with religious fervor in the heliocentric system." It was this nonconscious symbolic belief that "caused him to seek natural laws." And Pauli concludes, "it can be seen that in Kepler the symbolical picture precedes the conscious formulation of a natural law." [6]

This is very closely in accord with Kekulé's opinion that new truths often do not originate with the evidence but with an image that comes in advance and brings a fore-visioning of the form the answer is eventually to take. Such images, Pauli remarks, contain a "strong emotional content" and they are *not thought out but beheld."* [7] They are placed there by the depths of the psyche as in a dream or a reverie, as the flow of imagery fills the mind of the scientist speculating about his subject.

These images that come to the fore must then be related to the objective data that are being studied; and they must be related also to the special conceptions prevailing at the time, as well as to the general framework of contemporary thought. And when all these connections have been satisfactorily accomplished so that a new insight has been gained, something happens that reaches beyond the scientific search for truth. Pauli speaks here from his own experience of "the reaction of the knowledge gained on the gainer of that knowledge." [8] To achieve a union between a psychic image and the ob-

[6] *Ibid.*, pp. 170-171.
[7] *Ibid.*, p. 153, my italics.
[8] *Ibid.*, p. 212.

jective subject matter has a profoundly moving effect upon the person who has brought the union about.

The act of discovery in science, objective though the scientific criteria for it may be, is an event of great *personal* significance for the scientist. It has personal meaning for him in many small ways, in terms of the satisfaction of accomplishing something tangible in his work, or in terms of the personal vanity that comes with increased recognition and success in one's profession; but these are of secondary consequence. The major effect takes place in the depths of the psyche, for, in Pauli's words, "the process of knowing is connected with *the religious experience of transmutation* undergone by him who acquires knowledge." [9]

What does this *religious experience* involve? Let us consider what has taken place to make it possible.

In the modern age the scientist has carried the banner of creative personality. He has done this inadvertently, for the style of thinking that goes with the scientific attitude has tended to emphasize objectivity and to deprecate personality. Nonetheless, despite himself, the scientist has shown himself to be a creative type. He has become both an embodiment and a symbol of the creative faculties of personality in modern man.

Creativity is not reserved, however, for any single style of personality. It is not the special and distinctive province of the scientist any more than it is reserved for the artist, the businessman, or the mother caring for her family. Creativity is rather a quality of the psyche in

[9] *Ibid.*, p. 212, my italics.

the course of its natural growth. It is a quality of whole-ness emerging in the midst of the individual's quest for life.

The quest for life is the starting point and the original source of energy in the organism. At an earlier point in our discussion we spoke of this as the *survival drive* inherent in all the forms of protoplasm. It is life moving ever toward its own continuation, altering its forms, but ever extending itself. The patterns that provide the forms and directions for this movement of life derive from the organic psyche, for the organic psyche acts as the organ of meaning and of protoplasmic guidance toward survival in the human species. It draws the life process forward with imagery of many kinds, but the most fundamental of these images are the dynatypes; for these are the im-ages that provide the characteristic forms and the nec-essary energy for the development of individuality in particular lines of activity.

The dynatype of the scientist is expressed as the image of the seeker for truth in nature. The roots of this are deep in the individual form of his organic psyche. As they grow, drawing the dynatype toward maturity, they carry the whole personality toward greater development. The enactment of the dynatype takes place in the outer world, in society. Its expressions are embodied likewise in outer works, in tangible objects and activities. But the source of all this is within the person, for it is the directive images, the dynatypes, that move the process along, guide it, and shape it.

The energy available to the dynatype is survival energy.

It derives from the protoplasmic urge toward the purposeful extension of life. In its activity and in its frustration, both of which could be seen in our discussion of the experiences of August Kekulé, it arouses images of many types and patterns from the depths of the psyche. These images provide models for cognition. They are present and potential as available forms in which the outer world can be interpreted and understood. These are the cognitypes. Their source is in the depths of the organic psyche, and their function is to provide forms by which the outer world can be made meaningful to man, useful, and significant for the furtherance of his drive toward the extension of life.

In this process, there is a continuing interplay between the outer material which is to be studied or worked with, and the images within the psyche. The outer material presents a constant challenge. By itself it is meaningless; but if the images do not conform to it, they also will be meaningless. The outer material draws the images down to earth and anchors them. At the same time, it itself is elevated and elaborated by the cognitypes, deriving from them its meaning for life. Neither is of value without the other. But to join them and to blend them in a way that does justice to both and permits each to enhance the other is the most difficult and challenging, and ultimately the most creative act of all.

It is an act of unification, drawing the inner and the outer together to form a new entity that will be meaningful and useful for life. When this is achieved, outer reality is no longer impersonally separate from the human being.

It has been joined to him through the action of his psyche. The images have made the outer object a meaningful part of him, and he now permanently belongs to the new entity. For it is his art work. It is the outer opus that embodies the inner striving of his personality.

To imprint upon material reality the mark of the deep psyche and to make it thus meaningful in a new way is the essence of art. In this sense it is ever the goal of the creative scientist, who is indeed an artist. By its very nature, it is much more than a technical work in which the outer material is reshaped by the creative person. It is an act of integral relationship, a joining of the inner person with the outer world, each impregnated by the other. It is an act of wholeness, for it reaches beyond the opposites of life. It reaches beyond the division separating the psychologic and the physical, and it brings about an experience of unity as the imagery of the psyche is concretely embodied in an opus in the world. With this, the separateness of entities in nature is transcended in an act of unification; and this becomes an experience of sacramental proportions for the scientist who achieves it.

Such acts of wholeness, which the scientist brings about as a creative person, are indeed religious events. And this is as it must be, for the drive of the dynatype behind them expresses an essentially religious dedication. In achieving it, the scientist fulfills himself not merely as a scientist but as a human being. In bringing about a union between the outer material and the inner image, thus establishing a condition of wholeness in the world, he is by that act living wholeness within himself. In that moment he is granted a rare opportunity to feel the personal impact of unity as a fact of life. The act of creative discovery thus becomes for him an experience of truly spiritual realization. It is indeed, as Pauli has told us, a moment of transformation, a moment when the intellectual separateness of the scientist is transmuted into a profound, unifying sense of connection to life.

There is much that we can learn in pondering the significance of such events. But are we as individuals able to appreciate what is personally involved here? *Can we recognize that such acts of wholeness comprise one of the major new forms that religious experience is taking in the modern age?* When we have truly grasped the implications of these experiences of unity we shall at last be able to break down the dualistic barriers that have been separating science from the life of the spirit. With this also we shall be able to re-establish our contact with the creative resources of individual existence and open the way for a spiritual renaissance of personality in the very midst of our scientific world.

10 * *Evolution in modern existence*

MAN'S CAPACITY FOR SELF-TRANSFORMATION

In the preceding chapters we have described some of the signposts along the way of the long journey which comprises the growth of human personality. What a distance has been covered from man's emergence out of the trial and error of natural evolution to his creative moments of scientific discovery and his transforming experiences of unity! The distance is indeed so great as to cause us to wonder whether the men who first banded together in the wilderness belong to the same breed as men like Einstein and Schweitzer, who have penetrated and participated in the mysteries of the cosmos.

A close look is enough, however, to convince us that they do all belong to the same species. We have only to notice how their relatives behave! While we honor the qualities of such men as Smuts and Pauli and Schweitzer, we cannot fail to observe the behavior of their countrymen, who spring from the same stock as they. These display a marked resemblance to the men who flourished in the primeval forest. And so we could conclude that, after all, the human species has not changed fundamentally. Nonetheless, the feeling persists that something *is* different. In some form evolution *has* been taking place in the course of civilization. Our task now is to discover what that form is, and what its significance is for modern man.

For clues to the continuity of evolution in modern civilization, let us recall the perspective we have considered in the course of this book. We took as our starting point the basic dictum of natural science that man is a part of the physicochemical world, that he arises from the animal kingdom. This conception plays a fundamental role in modern man's thinking. It is in fact so basic a belief that he takes it for granted and considers it to be a self-evident truth, an unquestionable canon of common sense. In the eyes of *modern man* anyone with the slightest intelligence must recognize that human beings belong to the animal kingdom; and thus if we wish to communicate with *modern man* seriously and sympathetically upon other aspects of human life we have to begin by accepting the naturalistic preconceptions concerning the nature of man.

That is one important reason why we took a biological

point of view as the starting point for our discussions in this book. But there is another, more objective reason that should not be minimized. It is simply the fact that the creative spirit in man can be recognized most clearly, can be understood most adequately, and developed most constructively when it is studied within a framework that meets the criteria of science.

Studying man as part of nature, we went with Edmund Sinnott back to the ultimate formless stuff of the life process. We turned our attention to protoplasm itself, and there we observed that as protoplasm is embodied in individual organisms it works always toward a purpose that inheres in the form of its particular organism. It seems always to direct itself toward goals that express the nature of the species in which it is manifested. These are life goals; they are goals whose fulfillments tend toward the continuation and extension of life, not only in the individual organism but in the world at large. It is as though protoplasm is the bearer of a large and ongoing process, a process of life that is, on the one hand, the underlying principle of all existence, and on the other hand the specific goal and meaning of individual lives.

This twofold aspect of protoplasm holds a large significance. Its operation is both personal and more than personal. Protoplasm works for the extension of life in general, but it does so only in individual forms, in the form of an ameba, in the form of a fish, in the form of a human being. All these contribute to the life process as a whole, but each does so by working toward its special goals in accordance with its organic structure. Each enacts its unique pattern of life, unfolding the possibilities inherent in its existence. The life of organisms thus presents a progressive unfoldment of potentialities by which the individuals of each species *become* what their protoplasmic nature makes it possible for them to *be*.

The protoplasmic process of life moves forward into the future toward goals that embody the specific purposes of life for each organism. Thus the bird builds its nest to provide for the procreation of life; and correspondingly the artist among human beings constructs his art work as also an extension of life within his qualitative frame of reference. Whatever their specific nature, these protoplasmic purposes are presented to the organism as guiding images that draw activity forward. In lower animal species we can detect these images only by inference and implication; we can only say that images are working there *in principle*. But in the human species we have ample indication of the presence and importance of imagery. This is because of the higher level of differentiation and development in man's psychologic capacities.

The images that derive from man's protoplasmic nature can actually be visualized, or perceived in other forms, and brought to consciousness. Either they present themselves directly or, more usually, because they carry the qualities of the organic depths of the psyche, they are represented in symbolic forms. When their imagery is visualized by the inner eye of the psyche, in dreams, in fantasies, or visions of other kinds, it becomes possible for them to be described, communicated, studied, and discussed. In this we saw the source of the imagery of poetry, painting, and the plastic arts. In addition, as it is brought to the level of verbalization, the imagery of the human psyche is able to be articulated, enlarged upon, extended, and varied in ways that relate it constructively to the outer aspects of life. We saw this process at work in the realm of scientific discovery, and it is present in principle in many other areas of civilized life.

This is our key to what the psyche is. It is that special organ that presents and develops the goals of man's protoplasmic nature. The psyche is thus *the organ of meaning and direction in human life*. It is that aspect of protoplasm that draws forward the growth of the entire organism in terms of the purposes implicit in protoplasm itself.

The psyche is the bearer of those goals that channel man's activities in the direction of survival, first in basic biologic forms and then in advanced qualitative forms. The psyche is the carrier also of the unfulfilled potentialities of man's life. It contains the possibilities for growth that are inherent in the individual organism but which remain latent there, awaiting an enlargement in man's awareness of himself before they can become realities in his existence.

Above all else, the psyche is, like protoplasm, a process. It is ever in movement. Thus when we spoke of the protoplasmic imagery of the psyche we drew particular attention to its quality of ongoingness, its flow. It is by the flow of imagery out of the depths of the organic psyche that ever-new meanings are made available for man's life experience.

In this lies the great fertility of the psyche, its tremendously affirmative and constructive quality. As the psyche is the image-making faculty of the human organism, it is correspondingly the meaning producing faculty as well. The images are the raw materials out of which meanings are made. By its nature the psyche is inherently productive and inherently growing. Thus, unless its natural flow is constricted by impasses of conflicting wills within the person or by the inhibiting effect of social conventions, it moves freely forward and opens ever larger areas of meaningful activity. In this way the potentialities of man's existence expand from within as the protoplasmic life process draws the organic psyche toward a fuller realization of its potentialities.

This general conception, which is a fundamental theoretical formulation, has important practical consequences for the individual interested in developing the capacities of his personality. To realize that the meanings and possibilities of man's existence derive from the processes of his protoplasmic nature provides a key to what the ultimate goals of psychological work are; and it indicates to us also what we can legitimately hope to achieve by disciplined work in the depth of the psyche.

The ultimate goal of psychological work is to draw the processes of the psyche forward so that more of their imagery, more of their implicit purpose becomes available for the wholeness of the person's life in the world. Then what is latent as potentiality at the protoplasmic depth of the psyche can come forth to grow and bear its fruit. More of that dark wisdom that is part of man's protoplasmic nature can then also become accessible to consciousness via the cognitypes. Then it becomes concretely possible for man to *know,* as Alfred Adler said, more than he *understands;* for the process of cognition then proceeds darkly and directly out of the flow of imagery at the depths of the organic psyche.

The deeper we go into the seed of man's protoplasmic wholeness, the more this knowing comes forth to shed its light upon our lives; and at each step it adds new testimony to our realization that man's spiritual nature is inherent in the protoplasmic core of his being. It enables us to recognize that man is a member of the animal kingdom whose distinguishing characteristic is his perception and experience of meaning in the world.

Man draws the meaning of his life out of the depths of his human nature. The significance of his existence is present implicitly in the very structure of his being, but it discloses itself only in symbolic forms. By means of the symbols that arise out of the protoplasmic depths of his psyche, man reaches out to connect his individuality with the encompassing unity and ongoingness of the life process as a whole. As man identifies himself with the symbolic meanings that come to him from within, he enters into a more fundamental, supportive dimension of his existence. As he experiences the reality of this, as he enacts these images in his life, he is enlarged and even transcends himself; for his activities then establish an inner connection to the encompassing wholeness of life. Here man touches the sustaining dimension of human existence, and the channel through which he reaches it is the imagery of the organic psyche. The symbolism of the deep psyche provides the patterns by which man's connection to the larger dimensions of life becomes a fact of his existence.

With this experience, a most significant stage is reached in the progressive movement of evolution. The human species has arrived at its present level of development by the same process of biological selection that has determined the qualities of all the other species in the animal kingdom. But the human species is different from all others in one most important respect. Man alone has *the capacity for self-transformation,* the ability to redirect his existence through the development of resources that are part of his organic nature.

This is the capacity that belongs to the psyche. From it come the purposes and meanings of man's activities, and the psyche provides them in infinite variation. The psyche is the medium by which significant change enters man's life; it is the channel through which new perspectives become part of his understanding and his activity. Inevitably so, for in human beings the psyche is the organ of growth with respect to *meaning* in experience. New goals and new directions enter life by means of it. The psyche is thus the organ of growth for the individual human being who is working to fulfill the potentialities of his personal existence; and it is the organ of growth for mankind as a whole, for mankind considered as a species in the context of natural evolution. By the development of his psychologic capacities man raises himself above the basic condition in which he first emerged as a distinct species. The psyche is the organ with which he makes his additions to the natural process of evolution, carrying evolution forward within his individual existence, and extending the meaning of his life.

In this we see one of man's most remarkable characteristics. Other species are able to become only what it is their specific nature to be: the bee builds its hive ever in the same way, the bird her nest, the beaver his dam, and so on; but man's capacities hold an infinity of never-ending possibilities. The fulfillment of these possibilities, what is spoken of in religious and philosophic contexts as the "perfection" of man, is achieved through the disciplined development of the capacities of his psyche.

SPIRITUAL DISCIPLINES FOR SURVIVAL

A very interesting understanding of this was demonstrated by the Midrashic rabbis. In a perceptive text of the Midrash, it is written, "And Isaac asked the Eternal: 'King of the World, when Thou didst make the light, Thou didst say in Thy Torah that the light was good; when Thou didst make the extent of the firmament and the extent of the earth, Thou didst say in Thy Torah that they were good; but when Thou hadst made man in Thine image, Thou didst not say in Thy Torah that man was good. Wherefore Lord?' And God answered him, 'Because man I have not yet perfected, and because through the Torah man is to perfect himself, and to perfect the world.' " [1]

What a subtle awareness of man's place in evolution is expressed in that commentary on the book of Genesis! All the other species in the animal kingdom have come as far as their specific natures make it possible for them to come. Man alone possesses the capacity of taking steps beyond the limitations of the form in which he was created. Man has the ability to perfect himself, to develop himself beyond his primary evolutionary form. Indeed, it is more than a capacity but a responsibility, for what God requires of man is that he work toward perfection until he achieves it.

And what, according to the Midrashic rabbis, is the tool with which man is to achieve his perfection? It is the Torah. The Torah in the restricted meaning of the term is the first five books of the Old Testament, the Five Books of Moses. But in the wider use of the term in the Hebraic tradition, the Torah is the total body of teachings concerning the principles of human conduct disclosed first to Moses and then to succeeding generations engaged in the study and amplification of the Mosaic Law. The word, Torah, in fact, is often used to mean truth in general, especially that kind of truth that concerns man's underlying nature and the ultimate purposes of his life in relation to God. In this sense the Midrashic text is telling us that man's task in the world, the purpose of his life as God requires it of him, is that he use his

[1] Quoted by Edmond Fleg in *The Life of Moses*, London, Gollancz, 1928, pp. 137, 138.

knowledge of spiritual principles in order to fulfill those potentialities within him left incomplete when he was first created as a species, or, to put it in the modern vernacular, when he emerged in his present form out of the flux of evolution.

The meaning and goal of man's life is that he fulfill within himself the potentialities of existence that are present in the seed of his organic nature. Fulfilling these, man draws himself beyond the boundaries of biologic structure that encompass the animal kingdom. He achieves that act of "self-transformation" that the religious texts describe as the "perfection" of man. He fulfills what was possible for him and moves onto a new dimension of existence.

What are the means with which man shall achieve this? In each mature religion and culture man has been given, or has devised out of the depth of his nature, a special knowledge of the principles of spiritual growth that operate in human personality. Inevitably these systems of knowledge are couched in terms and concepts that derive from the general world view of their particular civilization. They therefore carry the marks of their traditions and of the special circumstances of culture and history in the midst of which they were born.

Very often, also, such systems of knowledge are deliberately made esoteric, lest individuals who are not able to understand their implications misuse them. And because of the subtlety and elusiveness of the subject matter itself, such systems of spiritual knowledge are often presented symbolically, their meanings concealed by an imagery that can be comprehended only by the person who has been initiated into its mysteries. They are symbolic also because the perceptions of life which they express are not achieved by the rational intellect, but are the product of the nonrational depths of the psyche. Cognition at that level comes by imagery rather than by analysis, and the knowledge that reflects the self-awareness of the processes of the organic psyche is therefore bound to be presented in symbolic forms. It is this symbolic insight into the principles of man's spiritual growth that needs, in our time, to be penetrated by scientific understanding in order that it can be translated into terms that can be incorporated into the experience of modern man.

The *Torah* of which the Midrashic rabbis spoke is such a body of symbolic insights interpreting the fundamental processes of man's inner life. Specifically, the term *Torah* refers to the knowledge of spiritual principles in man's life as that knowledge has grown within the framework of the Mosaic tradition. It seems, however, that each civilization that reaches some degree of maturity develops a *Torah* of its own, an indigenous system of spiritual knowledge and teaching that describes, within the frame of reference of its own cultural life experience, the principles by which the human personality grows toward wholeness.

These systems present a symbolic set of concepts with which individuals can interpret the dynamic factors working within their lives, factors often personified as *powers* in animistic views of the world. And they describe also specific methods of working toward the ultimate goals of personality achievement within the horizons of their understanding. Such procedures for personal growth are sometimes merely suggested and left to the discretion of the individual; at other times they are made obligatory for the entire community. Very often, too, the procedures recommended for spiritual growth are ritualized and symbolized and so are encased in a system of religious practices in which the observance of ritual details obscures and eventually negates its underlying aims.

The essence of all such symbolic systems of teaching about the nature of man is that they seek to direct the human being toward a greater degree of growth in his individual existence. They seek to open a way toward a larger fulfillment, or, in their nonscientific, spiritual language, toward a "perfection" of man's potentialities.

This development in man's capacities which they seek is not exclusively religious. Often the goal of such disciplines and ritual procedures is a larger capacity of awareness of personality specifically for use in the hunt, or in warfare, or in carrying out particular social roles in the life of the family or the community as a whole. The goal of the techniques of Zen Buddhism, for example, as historically practiced in Japan, is not limited to the religious development of the personality. It is intended rather to enlarge the capacities of the individual in all areas of his experience. Zen practices have thus been utilized to give the Samurai warriors a greater freedom for self-sacrifice in battle, and to give active men in the social order, such as political leaders and businessmen, a freedom from personal concerns and a stimulus in their work. It has been used as well to induce that feeling of creative spontaneity that is necessary for the peculiar combination of freedom and conventionality that is found in the writing of Japanese poetry; and it has been used also as a basis for participation in such artistic arrangements of social life as the tea ceremony, the placement and display of flowers, the practice of swordsmanship and archery.

Throughout the varieties of the so-called "primitive" religions, one finds abundant instances in which techniques for the larger development of the faculties of personality are used in the service of specifically social goals. The Shamans or medicine men use their methods of influencing the state and quality of their consciousness, not for personal religious purposes only, but for the conduct of life in the community as a whole.

The same is true of the varieties of Yoga practices within Hinduism. The highest use of these, within the scale of Hindu values, is for the ultimate achievement of spiritual unity and the attainment of *Nirvana*. But by far the majority of Hindus use Yoga techniques for purposes that fall far short of that ultimate goal. The outcome of yoga practices for these people is that the capacities of their personalities are enlarged in ways that are reflected in their social conduct. We see, therefore, the strong influence of yoga doctrines and yoga practices in the lives of many of the persons who have held positions of leadership in Hindu civilization: and we are bound to observe also that the traditional yoga conceptions seem to be in need of significant adaptation if they are to meet the challenges of modern industrial society.

Considering the variety of religious doctrines that work toward the disciplined development of the psychologic capacities of the personality, it is interesting to note that one of the most succinct statements of their essence and purpose is found in the Old Testament. There, Moses summarized in a most direct and trenchant way the reasons for which the Torah had been given to the people. You are to follow these teachings, he is reported to have said to the Children of Israel, "in order that you may *live* and not die."

The purpose of the Torah, and of other comparable systems of spiritual instruction that use ritual observance for a creative purpose, is to bring about *an extension of life* for the group to whom the teaching has been given, given, that is, ostensibly by God. This would mean that the purpose of such doctrines of belief and practice is *survival,* survival in the twofold meaning of which we spoke in an earlier portion of this book.

In one aspect its goal is basic biologic survival, and to appreciate the importance of this we must remember how precarious is man's life in the rudimentary conditions of culture in which the basic religious conceptions were first formulated. In those circumstances the more efficient and orderly organization of a society regulated by religious dicta, and especially with stringent rules for hygiene in a premedical age, made an important contribution to the continuance of life. But the second aspect of survival was even more meaningful. This was the qualitative survival, the feeling that the ongoingness of life is to be judged not merely biologically but in terms of meaning.

The Mosaic statement that the purpose of the Torah was to enable the people "to live and not die" involved both of these aspects of survival. It would bring a greater physical survival with its sensible teachings concerning the conduct of life with respect to both health practices and social ethics. But it promised a qualitative survival of much larger significance when it said that if the Children of Israel carried out the spiritual teachings of the Torah, *not only* would their physical lives be more productive and more comfortable, but also that they would have an important role in the future history of the world.

This role must be understood as a mythical promise and as one that is found in equivalent terms in many another system of religious belief. Its essential meaning is that if the particular people to whom the spiritual teaching has been given (in this case the Children of Israel) will carry out the discipline with dedication, they will become a model among the nations of the world. The other nations, seeing their prosperity, will seek to emulate them by doing as they do, that is, by following the same principles of spiritual discipline; and in doing this they will fulfill the purpose that was in the Mind of God when He presented the teachings to the people in the first place.

This is the conception that underlies the teaching of Moses by which he was undertaking to make a nation of "priests," a nation of spiritually developed persons who would be a model for other nations, out of a simple, apparently untutored people. This goal of eventually raising the spiritual level of all mankind involved an extension of the life principle in qualitative terms, in terms of meaning. In the Mosaic prophecy which is attributed to the last years of Moses, it is said, however, that this goal would come to naught if the Children of Israel failed to follow the principles of the Torah. For then they would not develop themselves to the point where they would be models and inspirations for the other nations, and so the other nations would not follow their spiritual lead. But if they did hold to the teachings of the Torah, they would reach a high point of human development, and they would by their example lead all of mankind to spiritual heights as well.

In this context we can see the significance of the statement of the Midrashic rabbis, which we have cited. If man follows a system of spiritual teaching (in this case the Biblical Torah, the Five Books of Moses) he will bring about a larger growth in his human capacities. He will move further toward that "perfection" of which the rabbis spoke. And in doing this he will display the capacities that are peculiar to his being a member of the human species, for he will manifest the fact that the capacity for transforming his primal traits and transcending them is an integral part of human nature. Man is inherently a being in growth. The need for growth is in his very structure and it requires him to carry life further than the form in which he found it. Other animal species, we have noted, are able to fulfill themselves only within the narrow limits of their instinctual patterns of behavior. They can become no more than what they were made to be. The creation of man, however, was never completed, so the rabbis tell us, and so man's life is open in its possibilities. God fashioned the human being up to a certain degree, and then left man to do the rest himself, to "perfect" himself by his own efforts. Thus it is that the human species alone is able to and is free to move beyond the qualities with which the evolutionary process originally endowed it.

THE SUSTAINING DIMENSION OF EXISTENCE

What are the implications of drawing together these two diverse lines of thought, the intellectual, naturalistic way of selective evolution and the intuitive, symbolic way of the Midrashic rabbis? In the perspective of evolution we saw how protoplasm, even in its primal forms, involves a factor that directs it from within. We could identify this, in principle if not in fact, as the psychic component in protoplasm. This psychic component enlarges itself and becomes increasingly important as protoplasm appears in more advanced forms in the course of evolution. By the time it has reached the human level of life, it has developed to the point where it is an intricate, self-consistent, constructive, actively functioning part of the total organism.

This is the point in the process of evolution at which it becomes possible to discern the organic psyche as a distinct and dynamic reality in the human being. It is the directive principle working toward growth in the individual and it is also the source of creative meaning in his existence. With the development of the organic psyche, therefore, large new possibilities open in the life of man. The psyche is the organ of growth as growth is guided from within. It emerged as a part of nature, as proto-plasm was engaged in extending the life process. And with it the life process does indeed extend itself, even transform itself. For when the process of evolution brought forth the organic psyche in man, it was creating an instrument with which the entire biologic process of life could one day transcend itself. The movement and growth of the organic psyche provides the means by which the process of evolution can take a step forward, can move beyond itself from within itself, by means of the life growth within individuals of the human species.

With this understanding it becomes possible for us to recognize the ultimate evolutionary significance of re-ligious systems that provide disciplines for the psychologic development of personality. They are continuing the process of evolution within man, and thus their spiritual dedications are actually extensions of the life process transferred to a higher dimension. Those individuals who reach a high level of achievement with these spiritual procedures, the saints, the mahatmas, the holy ones in each tradition, are persons who have actually carried the evolutionary process of life further within their individ-ual existence than nature herself had taken it. In the words of the Midrashic rabbis again, since man's creation was left by God as an uncompleted act, it has remained for man himself to complete his own creation, and this by "perfecting" himself. Most human beings have neglected this task, but those individuals in mankind's history who have dedicated themselves to this work have been exalted in two ways: firstly, their lives have become channels for nature through which the processes of evolution could continue their progressive movement; and secondly, they have also become channels through which the purposes of God's creation could be drawn closer to fulfillment, as they have worked toward the perfectibility of man within their own existence.

As we perceive this, there comes a major implication which we should not overlook. This is our realization that the extension of evolution in man's life involves a disciplined work directed toward developing capacities that are latent in the depths of the psyche; and further, that the high development of these capacities seems always to open a contact with a dimension of reality that transcends human existence, that transcends it and in some ineffable way underlies it as well.

What seems to take place is an experience of connection with a sustaining dimension of life. As a large development of the depth capacities of the psyche is achieved, this dimension becomes increasingly available to the individual, transmuting the quality of his existence and enlarging the scope of his outward experience. Sometimes this sustaining dimension is identified as a personal god, and sometimes it is not. The forms of it vary widely with the time and place in history. It would seem, in fact, that the specific names by which it is called and the categories with which it is described are of secondary importance. Something underlies all this, sustains and pervades all this, and whatever this dimension of existence is, it is what opens to man and becomes manifest in his life when he disciplines and develops the capacities latent in the depths of his organic psyche.

With this we come to a simple insight, and yet one that can have tremendous practical importance in our time. We have observed the profound ambivalence that is experienced by modern man at the present juncture of Western civilization. He has a long history of symbolic religious experiences behind him, and yet they are not available to him as effective spiritual principles that will work now in his life.

Why have they lost their power? The reason is not to be found on a metaphysical level. The position of God in the created world remains the same as it ever was, and the messianic principle of salvation is as potentially transforming an experience as it ever has been in history. The religious facts are the same, but the symbolic forms that carried the facts and made it possible for them to be experienced intensely, intimately, and in depth, no longer function with the same strength. It is as though the old symbols have worn themselves thin, and so are no longer adequate to carry the weight of the fundamental experiences that connect man to the fullness of life.

If this is so, and if we are correct in saying that it is not that the ultimate facts of God and Salvation have changed but only that the symbolic carriers of these facts have broken down in Western civilization, the reason why old spiritual principles have lost their power must be sought on a psychologic level. What is required is a large enough frame of reference and a method by which the psychologic contact with the primary spiritual principles can be restored. Then their inherent power will become evident again as a fact in man's life.

What kind of frame of reference and what kind of method can do this? Here the way of holistic depth psychology may be of considerable help.

The wisest commentators of our time, Tillich, Buber, and Toynbee, Mumford, Sorokin, and Jung, have called attention to the fact that the symbols which have traditionally been the carriers of the sense of the presence of God and the workings of salvation for the individual soul do not function well in modern civilization. In our time those symbols are very seldom able to draw forth experiences that shake the person until he finds his root in a bedrock of reality, as they did, for example, in the day of Augustine. But today the primary religious facts that lie behind the symbols have a quality of unreality, as though they are not really taken seriously even by the persons whose professional interest it is to talk about them.

This condition is a psychological fact, and as a result of it modern man has not been able to achieve that connection to life that would unify his existence in terms of both the macrocosm around him and the microcosm within him. A further aspect of this and one of the characteristics of a psychologic situation in which the symbolic representations of spiritual principles no longer carry the conviction of ultimate meaning is that they become doctrines and concepts to be intellectually discussed and disputed about. Then it is that even the most fundamental facts of spiritual experience—God, Being, Messiahship—are reduced to nothing more than words. At that point the psychologic condition has reached an impasse, and a serious incapacity has arisen where religious experience is concerned.

To overcome it, it is necessary to take radical action. It is necessary to drop the confusing concern with traditional religious concepts—at least to drop it for a preliminary transitional period—and to adopt instead the metaphysically neutral standpoint of the organic psyche. We have taken note of the fact that, while man is a member of the animal kingdom, certain individuals in various cultures and periods of history have been able to achieve a level of personal development that reaches beyond the ordinary capacities of the human species. Such individuals carry the process of evolution forward within their own lives by fulfilling more of what is potential in man's organic nature; that is, in the phraseology of religion, by "perfecting" man within their individual existence they carry out the implicit purpose of God's creation. Such individuals, we observed also, achieve a contact and a unity with that dimension of being that underlies and sustains man's existence. In each case they accomplished this within the framework of a particular religious system. The fact, however, that such individuals have merged out of opposing religious conceptions indicates that the doctrines themselves are not of primary importance. Something more fundamental underlies the various religious conceptions and is the basis of the advanced experiences that stand out as beacons in history and as crowning products of the processes of evolution.

We can at this point easily become involved in a discussion of what specifically this underlying principle is. Further, we can become involved in an intellectualistic discussion of how to define it. And eventually we could become involved in a theological discussion of what name to give it. But all of these would merely be symptoms of the psychological condition into which modern man has fallen, the psychological condition that obstructs larger spiritual growth. It would be an instance of how modern man, having lost his primal contact with the sustaining dimension of life, now further distracts himself by discussing the symbols of religious experience as though they were the spiritual principles themselves.

Our first task, then, is to establish a neutral ground from which we can work toward an authentic religious experience without making any unwarranted metaphysical or symbolic assumptions. To do this, it is necessary that we deliberately and carefully refrain from identifying ourselves with any special religious conception, and yet that we work with great intensity toward our goals of individual realization.

Paradoxical as it may seem, this is precisely the procedure that has been outlined in the historical texts in which the most advanced techniques of spiritual discipline are described. For example, the anonymous monk who wrote the fourteenth-century classic, *The Cloud of Unknowing,* recommended that a person who was engaging in this work of "spiritual striving" should divest himself of the emotional attachments that bind him to any special set of symbolic beliefs and observances. For the purposes of spiritual achievement, a person is not to prefer one rather than another. The reason is that all such differentiation becomes an impediment so that, as one engages in it, it thickens the cloud that separates man from the ultimate unity underlying his existence. The individual is rather to press downward beyond all these separations until he reaches that common ground in which all special beliefs and experiences have their origin. This is spoken of in *The Cloud of Unknowing* as man's "naked being." It is the core of his existence. When a human being achieves a unity with this core of *naked being* within himself, he is able to proceed toward the further experience of unity with God which is the stated goal of the work in *The Cloud of Unknowing*. After that he may return to his original and traditional beliefs; but now he will do so with a new, a transformed understanding of what lies behind them.

To a very large degree, what *The Cloud of Unknowing* speaks of as *naked being* corresponds to what we have spoken of here as the organic psyche. Both terms refer to the most fundamental, unconditioned ground of human experience. One important difference must, however, be noted. When we speak of the organic psyche we are introducing the modern awareness of dynamic processes that are at work in the depths of the human being. These are the processes by means of which the goals, the interior strivings that emerge out of the naked being of personality, are brought to fulfillment. The first step in the work of depth psychology is thus in accord with the primary goal in the work of *The Cloud of Unknowing*. It is to establish the ground of the individual's experience upon the deepest level of the organic psyche in terms of the unconditioned flow of protoplasmic processes. This is metaphysically neutral ground, for it provides a frame of reference within which the special symbolic forms by which these processes express themselves can be understood and utilized constructively. They can then be appreciated for what they are, revelations of meaning that arise out of the naked being of life, drawing man toward the extension and perfection of the life process by means of his personal existence.

The way to this central experience of one's organic psychic being is simple and direct. It requires essentially that the individual reach the point where he feels himself to be profoundly and spontaneously identified with the flow and growth of his organic psyche. Then the ultimate and intimate nature of his being can unfold and disclose itself in his existence, manifesting itself in many works and relationships in the outer world.

A variety of methods can be followed in working toward this experience of inner unity. They are not rigid techniques, and they cannot be applied in any set, predetermined pattern; nor is there any predictable regularity in their results. They are, however, procedures for reaching into the depths of man and establishing contact with reality there, as reality is mediated into human experience via the imagery of the organic psyche.

These procedures are used probingly and flexibly in the practice of holistic depth psychology in its attempt to help modern individuals recover a feeling of intimate participation in the wholeness and ongoingness of the cosmic life process. The framework of this book does not here permit us to enter into the details of these ways of working. They have, however, been discussed in considerable details in numerous seminars and workshops,[2] and this material is being prepared for publication with the illustrations and case material that the subject requires.

What is of primary importance in our present context, however, is that we comprehend the underlying principles that are the basis of these procedures. The goal toward which they are directed is the establishment of a sense of connection with the moving sources of life in such a way that the individual is able to know their reality by direct experience within the depths of his own being. These moving sources of life have an elusive, indeed an exasperatingly mercurial quality when we try to grasp them with the analytic intellect. Just when we think we have them firmly in hand, they slip through our fingers. How then can we know them? And most important, how can we encounter them directly? How can we make them a part of our intimate experience?

[2] Especially in conducting the 1958 meeting of the *Friends' Conference on Religion and Psychology* at Haverford College. It has also been dealt with in workshops at Wainwright House under the sponsorship of the Laymen's Movement, in seminars at the Drew University Graduate School, in lectures at the New School for Social Research, and in private seminars.

RELIGIOUS EXPERIENCE BEYOND DOGMA

Here we have what has seemed to be a most difficult question, and yet the basic approach to the answer is right at hand. Man has searched everywhere, all around himself, in his effort to make contact with the ultimate creative principles of the cosmos. He has cast about in the most distant and least accessible places, although, ironically enough, the knowledge he seeks is reflected within the depths of his own nature. To find it, he need only learn how to look within himself.

Why, indeed, is this so? And what are the forms in which the knowledge he seeks can be perceived?

When we spoke of the primal life stuff, of protoplasm, we noted that a directive principle is at work within the life process. This is the formative principle in protoplasm by means of which purpose and meaning enter the movement of life. These purposes and meanings are not visible on the surface of events. They work in the background of conscious activity and make their presence felt as silently guiding principles that are expressed, not in explicit conceptual form, but indirectly in terms of images. In this sense, what we have spoken of as the protoplasmic imagery that moves through the deep psyche of man is essentially *a series of reflections* of the dynamic principles and meanings directing the life process from its innermost parts. These reflections comprise the images that work in the depths of the psyche and enter life through dreams and visions and fantasies in ten thousand symbolic forms.

What we have just described is a reversible process, and this fact of its reversibility has important consequences for psychologic practice. Moving back through the varieties of symbolism that appear in the psyche, a person is enabled to reach down into the generic images in the depth of himself. These images are a series of reflections of the moving life process represented in symbolic forms at the protoplasmic level of the psyche. Here, indeed, an intimation of the nature and rhythm of life is given to man. Here a contact with life in its ongoingness becomes possible. And, most significantly, since this contact takes place within the depths of the human being himself, it involves inherently an *intimate participation* in the larger life process. Having worked psychologically back through the symbols and images to the core of naked being itself, the individual becomes one with the sources of his existence as these are immediately given within him.

With this, unity becomes a fact of experience, a reality of personal experience beyond all doctrinal beliefs and theological concepts. It is simply a fact of experience in itself, and its reality is attested by the enlargement of life, of awareness, and of capacities for effective living that it makes possible.

In the course of civilization, certain rare individuals have discovered for themselves the principles underlying this way of working, and have carried it to realization within the context of their life and times. Such persons stand out like beacons in man's history, for in their individual existence they have epitomized the possibilities of what a human being is able to become. Their manner of applying the principles of the psyche, as they intuitively perceived these principles, has been different in each case; but they have all had one characteristic in common. None has been able to fulfill the work by following a formula that was clearly stated in advance. Each has had to work probingly, even gropingly until the image of wholeness that was drawing him forward without conscious explanation would validate itself in ways that could not be foreseen. The procedures followed by others could be used only as suggestions or signposts; for ultimately all set procedures prove inadequate when they are tested by the uniqueness of the individual engaged in the work. Eventually each person finds himself engaged in an experiment in which he must somehow find the right relationship between the universal principles of the organic psyche and the requirements of his own unique existence.

Recognizing this fact, Mahatma Gandhi spoke in his monumental autobiography of his "experiments with truth." That phrase has a metaphysical sound, and the personal work that it involved together with its practical political consequences certainly had a religious significance to Gandhi. But the dynamic core of what Gandhi was doing was psychologic. He was engaged in a work of inner discipline which he practiced throughout his mature life in an effort to develop the capacities of his personality to the highest possible level.

Gandhi's personal aim was to achieve the fullest possible utilization of the faculties of his psyche; and in order to reach this goal he had to proceed as best he could, using this technique and that, prayer and fasting and meditation, and whatever other procedure was suggested to him by Hindu tradition, or by his knowledge of Christianity, Buddhism, and Mohammedanism, as well as by such modern authors as Tolstoy and Henry Thoreau.

Gandhi's work was experimental in a very rich sense of the word, for he tried all kinds of measures and methods, varying and altering them to find pragmatically what seemed to work best. The creative core of Gandhi's life thus comprises essentially a continuing discipline of psychological experiment conducted within himself.

The psychological goal of these experiments was the development and use of the latent faculties of the psyche, faculties that remain dormant in most human beings and are seldom awakened at all. Gandhi interpreted these psychologic entities in terms of his spiritual frame of reference, and he felt, therefore, that what his inner experiments were achieving was to bring him closer to God and to enable him to utilize "Soul-Force" in the world of men.

In The Cloud of Unknowing we find something very similar. There, experimental, psychologic techniques conceived in religious terms are practiced in order to reach a fuller development of the faculties of the personality.

Those persons in prescientific times who undertook the task of experimenting within themselves in order to enlarge their constitutional capacities of experience had to follow a procedure of trial and error until they could reach conclusions that would rest upon an empirical base. They were working experimentally with themselves, but they could not do their experimenting in the laboratory. Their personal lives had to serve as their laboratories. This, we should note, did not involve a sacrifice for them, but rather a commitment and a faith. They believed what modern man must still learn, that the work of enlarged personal development is a main road to the realization of meaning in life.

The prescientific experimenters in personality development turned their attention to what is the fundamental datum of psychological study: the processes of the psyche as it pursues its natural course of unfoldment toward wholeness. They were thus concerned with the experiences that take place within the holistic depths of human nature. They followed, in order to fulfill the purposes of their work, an experimental point of view.

They could not "control" their experiments in the modern sense. They could not repeat at will their "experiments in truth" with a single variable factor at a time. But they were able to observe the effects of their practices upon themselves, and within themselves. And they were able to discuss the effects of these practices with other individuals engaged in the work, comparing the results with one another, sharing their observations, and pooling their knowledge. It was thus that errors in the work could be eliminated; and though each "experiment" was individual, necessarily being limited to a single personality, the net result in each of those disciplines where there was some group continuity in practice was a crystallization of procedure that embodied an impartial consensus of judgment based upon trial and error.

In the course of the centuries during which men in various cultures and religious traditions have undertaken and recorded this kind of personal experiment, a considerable literature has accumulated. Taken together it comprises a large and fertile source of data for the empiric study of the depth processes of the psyche as experienced by individuals who approached the subject experimentally in the context of their particular symbolic view of the world and of reality.

This is the point at which we in the modern age with the intellectual equipment of a sympathetic depth psychology are in a position to make a substantial advance over the haphazard personal experiments of earlier generations. Since we have the accumulated records of the past available to us, we can study them objectively in the light of our modern depth conceptions with an awareness of the timeless significance of their original spiritual concerns. Now, with our fuller insight into the many dimensions of psychic symbolism, we can undertake to decipher their esoteric meanings in terms of the underlying processes in the holistic nature of man. We can then, using these written records as our empirical data, study them comparatively and critically so as to emerge eventually with a body of significant hypotheses conceived in the spirit of science.

Jacob Bronowski has defined science "as the organization of our knowledge in such a way that it commands more of the hidden potential in nature." In this sense, holistic depth psychology can become man's crowning science; for its very form and conception dedicates it to the development of more of the hidden potential in the nature of man.[3]

A science of man conceived in these terms would fulfill the basic need of modern man to understand the unity that links his animal nature and his spiritual aspirations. They are not separate entities, as has often been thought. They simply represent different stages in the inherent process of evolutionary growth. Those individuals who have carried the evolutionary process further than nature herself has brought it, who have continued the process of evolutionary growth within themselves by the use of special knowledge and disciplines, are prototypes of the creative spiritual being that modern man can become. They are instances of what Smuts speaks of as "holistic personality," and in them the ageless surgings of evolution find their fulfillment.

The particular value of holistic depth psychology in this area of experience is that it is not limited by particular metaphysical beliefs. It is able to work operationally and empirically in terms of the metaphysically neutral principles of the organic psyche: and it is able to draw the personality by means of these principles into connection with life at levels of existence that all mankind has in common.

Working upon this basic ground, depth psychology displays capacities of a special and most important kind. It seems to be uniquely equipped to serve as an intermedi-

3 Jacob Bronowski, *op. cit.,* pp. 14.

ary between the seed of divinity that is inherent in man and the sustaining dimension of existence, by whatever name this unnameable, abiding reality is called. In this realm, depth psychology clearly has a religious role to play in the life of modern man, even though it is not in terms of dogmatic religion.

The special calling of depth psychology is to reach beyond all special symbolic and metaphysical doctrines to the core of reality that underlies them. There the use of its special insights and procedures is to awaken the capacity for spiritual experience in modern man regardless of the special religious conceptions in which that experience will eventually be expressed. It does this in an essentially empiric way, for its emphasis is altogether upon what is actually experienced in the depths of the psyche rather than upon what is professed as a doctrinal belief. Further, and what is perhaps most significant of all, holistic depth psychology is able to work constructively at the core of religious experience precisely because it begins with a natural-science view of man. It sees the evolutionary meaning of man's life expressed in the fact that he is an organism whose nature requires spiritual growth in relation to the unifying processes of life. This spiritual growth involves a continuing relationship to the unifying processes of life, and it is upon this awareness that depth psychology bases its procedures for the development of personality.

It seems, now, as we reflect upon the original concern with which we undertook this book, that we have gone full circle to an opposite view of man's situation. While we began by calling attention to the emptiness of modern man's life and the imminent threat to his survival, we have found our way to a program of science and personal discipline that opens the way to significant advances in the evolutionary position of man.

These are indeed opposite extremes, and they may well seem incongruous when placed so close together. But both are valid, for the old saying that "extremes meet" is especially true of human life. Man's nature is to grow. When he is not able to grow, the dynamic life process that works within him doubles back upon itself and casts its energies into disorder. The result is confusion accompanied by the symptoms of disoriented living that have been diagnosed in modern times as *neurosis*. The choice before man is thus inherently one of extremes: either growth with its fullness of rewards in life or stalemate with growing restlessness, confusion, and eventual breakdown.

These extreme alternatives have been inherent in human life all through history, but modern technology and armament have multiplied the dangers and have made it all the more imperative that a road of growth be made accessible to modern man. It is at this point that depth psychology in its holistic form becomes more than a large frame of reference for scientific research. It becomes, much more, an urgently needed tool of survival for modern man because it provides an affirmative, scientifically grounded conception of man's life that can be used constructively in the creative development of human personality.

Both as critic of the old and as originator of new conceptions, Dr. Ira Progoff has long been in the vanguard of those who have worked toward a dynamic humanistic psychology. In his practice as therapist, in his books, as lecturer and group leader, as Bollingen Fellow, and as Director of the Institute for Research in Depth Psychology at the Graduate School of Drew University, he has conducted pioneer research and has developed major new techniques for the enlargement of human potential.

These studies have led to the founding of two significant organizations. The first is Dialogue House Associates which is devoted to using the *Intensive Journal* developed by Dr. Progoff as the basis for varied programs of personal growth in education, religion, industry, and social organization. The second is the Humanic Arts Research and Resource Center, which is devoted to developing experiential programs of advanced training for people who work in the helping and teaching professions.

The core of Ira Progoff's work is contained in a trilogy of basic books. *The Death and Rebirth of Psychology* (1956) crystallizes the cumulative results of the work of the great historical figures in depth psychology and sets the foundation for a new psychology of personal growth. *Depth Psychology and Modern Man* (1959) presents the evolutionary and philosophical perspectives, and formulates basic concepts which make creative experience possible. *The Symbolic and the Real* (1963) pursues the practical and religious implications of these ideas and applies them in techniques and disciplines which individuals may use in their personal growth.

Catalog

If you are interested in a list of fine Paperback
books, covering a wide range of subjects
and interests, send your name and address,
requesting your free catalog, to:

McGraw-Hill Paperbacks
1221 Avenue of Americas
New York, N.Y. 10020